HISTORY:
FACT AND FABLE

Willis Thornton

Dorset Press
New York

Published by Dorset Press,
a division of Marboro Books Corp.
1992 Dorset Press

ISBN 0-88029-763-8

Printed and bound in the United States of America
M 9 8 7 6 5 4 3 2

For Eugenia
who has a different
(and often a better)
way of approaching truth

Contents

MAN IS A BELIEVING ANIMAL, IT
has been said, and I think said truly.

He loves a good story. When he hears one, he desperately
wants it to be true. So he clings to his "good stories" in defiance of cold scholarship, even when the scholars find good evidence that they cannot be true.

History is encrusted with these glittering barnacles, to
which one applies the scraper of truth at his peril. Clio may
be the most austere and chaste of the Muses, but she has been
known to come down informally from Mount Helicon in a
mood so raffish that there are those who claim to have seen
her with her slip showing. And she *does* seem so much more
"folksy" when presented poetically by some folkloreate.

So anyone deserves about what he gets if he goes around
disillusioning people just for the fun of it, carelessly playing
the bull in people's china-shop of historical bric-a-brac. I
have, certainly, no such intent.

For I am well aware that the boy Lincoln was probably inspired and taught by the story about Washington and the
cherry tree, and that all the neat little anecdotes about Alfred
and the Cakes, Canute and the Sea, Bruce and the Spider, are

a means of teaching moral lessons to the very young which cannot be taught so well in any other way. I would even agree that it may be good for very small children to be taught implicit and literal belief in Santa Claus.

But it is something else to argue that he is a monster who tells a grown man that there is no Santa Claus. This is mere pleading for perpetual childishness, for the wistful reluctance to grow up that so often marks the American—a passionate clinging to youth that is also a rejection of maturity. I assume here that the reader has begun to put away childish things, or has left them behind; that he who stands every day face to face with life as it is can surely face life as it was.

We shall be discussing certain historical episodes and stories widely accepted as true and showing how scholars have either entirely refuted or cast grave doubts upon them. Yet there is no wish to break wantonly any cherished images; certainly none to be irreverent or smart-alecky. Many years of reading and researching in history have convinced me of this: that everything really fine and valuable in the great tradition that has come down to Western Civilization is set firmly on the bedrock of truth. It does not depend on the merely picturesque or melodramatic. The structure is just as solid, and even more beautiful, when it is stripped of its fretwork and ornamental mouldings.

For example, when I was a youngster, George Washington never appealed to me at all. He was a faraway figure on a pedestal, bearing no resemblance to real, flesh-and-blood people. It was not until I was able to divest him of some of the sugar-sculpture with which he had been encrusted that I got my first glimpse of the sheer strength of will and character that so firmly ruled a human being. That oily little child of the cherry tree had always stood squarely in the way. As a man I find far more admirable the Washington of the furious temper, which he (almost always) kept under such magnificent control, than the passionless plaster saint of the schoolboy stories.

It has been so with institutions and events. They are not less, but greater, when stripped of the gimcrackery of legend. It is only when the half-gods go that the gods arrive. A good deal of my own poking about in history has been due to a curiosity to get behind certain persons and events which seemed to me to have been presented with a certain cheap and too-easily-plausible glibness. And when, on a few occasions, I was able to arrive at something a little nearer the truth, I always found it to be not only more interesting, but more satisfying, providing a more solid foundation on which to build a regard for my country, my people, and mankind. The truth, I had found, was not only stranger than fiction, it was a better story altogether.

I should be the last to claim for the sketches that follow, any original research, any new discoveries, any real scholarship. They are stories, rather, of what better scholars than I have done to filter out from the stream of history the germ-laden muck of falsehood, as well as the sickish sugar-flavoring of cheap adulteration, and give us pure water to drink.

Those who delve into history have a vast and unending task not merely in discovering the facts, but in resolving the contradictions, lighting up the obscurities, and giving voice to the silences. It is like the building of a city—there is new construction, to be sure, but often the newer and better can be constructed only when false or shoddy building by past workmen has been torn down and cleared away. Like a thriving and growing city, the structure of history is never completed. There are always newer and finer structures of truth to be built on the sites of outmoded and discredited works, as well as structures of proved beauty and utility to be preserved against the attacks of time and man.

History is too important to be a fenced preserve for the professional historian. Intellectually curious people, though quite unprofessional, ought to read it, to study it, and on occasion to write it. And so I hope that some readers will be, as I myself have been, impelled to know more about these and other episodes in the never-exhausted story of man. That is why I have included, at the end of each episode, informal references to books which will lead the reader farther into the stories in which he finds a particular interest.

I should like to record my gratitude to Carl Wittke, historian, Professor of History and Dean of the Graduate School of Western Reserve University, whose student I once was, and who taught me how interesting history can be. Helpful and encouraging though he has been, he is in no sense responsible for the follies which I have no doubt committed. Miss Donna Root of the history division of the Cleveland Public Library has also been most helpful, as have numerous others whom neither space nor the probable limits of your patience permit me to mention.

WILLIS THORNTON

HISTORY:
FACT AND FABLE

The Boston Massacre of 1770

IT IS A HUNDRED TO ONE THAT the name Tonypandy doesn't mean a thing to you. But Josephine Tey, in her admirable book *The Daughter of Time*, is in a fair way to make it a general word for any historical event much exaggerated by the teller for his own purposes.

Tonypandy is a town in South Wales. There, according to Miss Tey, they still tell a shocking story of troops shooting down helpless miners. The episode is generally forgotten now; even histories of the labor movement in Britain do not mention it. But in Wales the word still passes: "Never forget Tonypandy." In this neighborhood, in 1910, there were bad labor troubles. Welsh miners were on strike, and violence was spreading throughout the Rhondda Valley. There was looting and destruction of property. Local police were unable to control the situation, and the Chief Constable of Glamorgan called on the central government for troops. Now it happened that the Home Secretary at the time was a man named Winston Churchill. He sent the troops, all right, but ordered them kept in reserve, meanwhile sending a body of Metropolitan Police to see what they could do first. These unarmed but well-trained police quickly got the situation under control, and Miss Tey avers that no soldiers ever came into contact with the crowd at all, let alone shot them down. But this did not prevent the rise of a lurid legend of subjection and slaughter.

Thus Miss Tey, at any rate. And she should be right, for she is much more than an ordinary writer of detective novels. Under the name of Gordon Daviot she has also written some well-researched historical novels and plays. So, coming on an historical episode whose reality was far less sensational than the popular belief in it, she calls it "Tonypandy."

America also has its Tonypandy. It is the "Boston Massacre." Now it is quite true that five men were killed and three others wounded in this affray. But the whole thing was far from a deliberate assault on peaceful unarmed civilians by a ruffianly set of blood-hungry soldiers, arousing righteous indignation which immediately distilled itself into the American Revolution. That is the Boston Massacre of the school books, the version fostered by Samuel Adams, that tireless and artful propagandist, who used it to serve his purposes. They were good purposes, as we look back upon them from a vantage point of 180 and more years later, and the ugly little affair in King Street served them well. But today we should be able to look back with a little more detachment; Josiah Quincy, counsel for the accused soldiers, was able even at their trial that same year to say, "We must not forget that we ourselves will have a reflective hour, in which we shall view things through a different medium—when the pulse will no longer beat with the tumults of the day—when the conscious pang of having betrayed truth, justice, and integrity shall bite like a serpent and sting like an adder. . . ."

Let us look back and see what we can see.

First, the affair happened after Boston had been for seventeen months occupied by the King's troops; it was no spontaneous flareup unconnected with other events.

Second, it happened on March 5, 1770, more than five years before Lexington and Concord.

Third, the British officers and soldiers involved were arrested and tried by the civil courts.

Fourth, a jury of Americans acquitted them, all but two, who were adjudged not guilty of murder, but guilty of manslaughter; and they were lightly punished.

Fifth, one of the victims made a dying confession that the mob provoked the firing, and that he was only amazed that the soldiers did not fire sooner.

Sixth, the sentry around whom the disorders developed was so anxious to avoid trouble that he vainly tried to retreat from his post in front of the Customs House to shelter within the building.

Seventh, no shot was fired until one of the British soldiers actually had his gun knocked out of his hands by a heavy stick or other missile.

Eighth, it is a tribute to the restraint both of the soldiers and the crowd that both were willing to withdraw from the scene after the shooting, thus avoiding what might have been a wholesale bloody slaughter.

Those are only a few points where the facts differ from the version known to the average school-child. Let us go back and see if we can determine a little more closely just what really happened. Fortunately the shorthand report of the *Trial of the British Soldiers* was published the same year of the trial, in Boston, and presents as fascinating a study of the reliability of witnesses, the passions which moved soldier and civilian, and of the sober, dignified proceedings of the trial as that of any similar proceeding I know. We shall here draw largely on the testimony and arguments in those hearings.

The soldiers had been ordered to Boston to back up customs and other officials who had been having difficulty in enforcing the laws, especially the unpopular revenue laws. When four full regiments had been sent, barrack facilities were inadequate, and it was found necessary to quarter the troops in warehouses within the town. This garrison was later reduced to two regiments, but the gesture was too late.

British regulars of 1770 were not exactly the flower of gentility. In our own times we have become accustomed to think of soldiers as a complete cross section of the people. But in 1770 the British regular army soldier was apt to be from the bottom layers of society. Those who came to Boston were such, and the women who followed the troops did little to endear them to the people of Boston. The soldiers were so poorly paid that it was customary for them to take odd jobs in off-duty hours to supplement their miserable pay. In fact, one of the conflicts in Boston arose from this circumstance. An American, obviously intent on provocation, asked one of the soldiers whether he would like some part-time work. Apparently in eager good faith, he replied that he would. "Then you can come and clean out my privy," said the American. The soldier was understandably indignant, and a fracas ensued, only one of many, in which several persons were hurt, and the soldiers forced to retire from the scene.

The presence of the troops in the streets, many of them direct from duty in disturbed Ireland, was a source of great annoyance to the Bostonians. There is good evidence that the movement to get rid of them was organized, and that clashes were provoked as a means of making their stay unbearable, in the hope that this would lead to their being withdrawn.

And if the British regulars of the 29th Regiment were pressed from the backwash of British society, it should be remembered that there were elements among the ropewalk workers and along the waterfront in Boston who did not exactly smell of attar of roses, either. Sam Adams is known to have been friendly with Andrew McIntosh, for instance, a brutal brawler and leader of a gang of waterfront toughs. Crispus Attucks, the white-Negro-Indian, was not wielding a cudgel for the first time on March 5, 1770. There is reason to believe that Sam Adams and others too genteel to engage in brawls themselves, encouraged the waterfront gangs to turn from bashing each other to the more satisfying game of badgering British soldiers.

In any event, clashes there were, and plenty of them. As Mercy Warren primly put it, in her *History of the Rise, Progress and Termination of the American Revolution, Interspersed with Biographical, Political and Moral Observations*, "Continual bickerings took place in the streets between the soldiers and the citizens; the insolence of the first, which had been carried so far as to excite the African slaves to murder their masters, with the promise of impunity, and the indiscretion of the last, was often productive of tumults and disorder that led the most cool and temperate to be apprehensive of consequences of the most serious nature."

The British troops set up virtually a military occupation. Guards challenged every person who entered or left the town by way of Boston Neck. The main guard was stationed directly across from the Boston Town House, with cannon pointing directly at the legislative chamber. British occupation officers justified all this on the ground that there had already been two small riots. There was a good deal of parading of troops in the streets to martial music, which Bostonians interpreted as a display to overawe them. Though the troops had orders to remain subordinate to the colonial civil government and to act only to back up the authority of magistrates, Bostonians felt that, potentially at least, a military despotism was fastening itself upon them. At least the Sons of Liberty were so convinced, and their activities in terrorizing Tories were not abated by the presence of the troops. The Whigs dominated the colonial legislature. But as long as the troops remained reasonably well-behaved and did not make good on the horrendous stories of atrocities that were passed from one person to another and appeared in the Whig newspapers, there was little chance of getting rid of them. Sam Adams filled his "Journal of Events" with racy descriptions of little boys being beaten in the streets by British regulars, gunfire and horse-racing on the Common on Sunday, and the enticement of Boston virgins. Very little of this seems to have been true, especially as regards the latter charge. A modern generation knows how difficult it is to prevent "fraternizing" between occupation troops and a local population, and in this case there was, of course, not only a common language, but all, soldiers and civilians, whether from Boston in Massachusetts or Boston in Lincolnshire, were British citizens. And then, as now, there were local girls who were not entirely immune to the charm of tall, dark, and handsome men in uniform. There was intermingling, and it caused scandal and bad-feeling, but there were no cases of the sort of forcible ravishment charged by the Whig propagandists. The troops, while they were a rough lot, especially those of the 29th Regiment, were kept under strict discipline.

But there were continual small incidents. Small boys, adept at pestering with saucy tongues, often goaded soldiers into threats or even punishment. Their tales, carried home (no doubt with embellishments), brought fathers to waylay soldiers off duty and to challenge them. Brawls would follow, and then on-duty soldiers would arrive to prick the citizens off the sidewalks with their bayonets. Ill-feeling snowballed, and soon between the Sons of Liberty and the troops a sort of running feud was being carried on. Personal bickering between particular citizens and particular soldiers sprang up, with hard words on either side. The soldier Killroy was heard to say that he longed for a good chance to fire on the unruly people, and this was duly reported and spread widely, though of course it was matched by similar threats by citizens.

Early in the spring of 1770 the pace of these incidents increased. One morning the town was plastered with notices that the soldiers were about to attack the populace, signed by a number of the British soldiers. The unlikelihood of any such notice being genuine escaped notice amid the rising passions of the day.

On the cold, moon-lit evening of Tuesday, March 5, Hugh White, a soldier of the 29th Regiment, was walking post in front of the Custom House in King Street. Such a guard had been maintained for months. It was a normal place for a guard, as the King's financial records and money were safeguarded there. A group of small boys appeared, jeering and throwing snowballs at White, the sentry. He threatened the boys, and gradually between fifty and sixty men gathered in the square, swinging clubs, and throwing pieces of ice, supplemented, some witnesses said, by clamshells. John Adams described them as "a motley rabble of saucy boys, negroes and mulattoes, Irish teagues and outlandish jack tars." Among them, swinging a club, was Samuel Gray, the man who had invited the British soldier to clean his outhouse, thus starting a brawl on the Saturday preceding. All manner of threats, taunts, and missiles were hurled at the sentry, who withdrew to the Custom House steps and knocked with the butt of his gun to gain entry. But no one opened and the sentry turned to face his tormentors, priming and loading his gun, and bringing it to a position of defense. "Fire! Fire, damn your blood, fire! You dare not fire!" yelled the crowd, pressing close.

No one could have blamed White very much if he feared for his life at this point. He called loudly for the guard.

From the nearby main guard post, relief came speedily, pressing through the crowd and pricking people out of the way with fixed bayonets. It was Captain Preston, the Officer of the Day, with a hastily gathered squad consisting of Corporal William Wemyss and seven men. They formed with White a little arc on the sidewalk in front of the Custom House. The gathering mob, intent on forcing an incident, faced the small knot of soldiers who were smarting under months of bickering and abuse, eager at once to teach the locals a lesson and to make their own position more secure and tenable. Captain Preston stood in front of his men to prevent their firing without orders, and repeatedly urged the crowd to disperse and go home.

Now the church bells began to ring (significantly, not only in Boston, but in several closely adjoining towns, suggesting advance planning). This was the usual signal for fire, at which everyone automatically turned out at night. People began streaming toward King Street, spurred by quick rumors of trouble. One witness, who had observed this turn-out of the citizenry, testified dryly that "they also cryed fire. I said it was very odd to come to put out a fire with sticks and bludgeons."

The mob in King Street grew, and as it grew, so did the throwing of pieces of ice, sticks, anything that could be found in the streets. The tumult grew louder, spiced with whistles, Indian yells, and every insult and taunt that could be dredged up, always daring the "bloody-backs" to fire. In nearby Dock Square a large crowd gathered and was harangued by a mysterious tall man in a white wig and a red cloak. No one reports what he said, but when he had finished, the crowd shouted for an attack on the main guard, broke up some market stalls for clubs, and dispersed, most of them joining the crowd already harassing the corporal's guard in King Street.

The mysterious tall man in the red cloak has never been identified, despite unsupported suggestions that it may have been Sam Adams himself. But he was evidently an agitator who egged on the mob and then disappeared. At the later trial, Justice Oliver told the jury, "I cannot but make this observation on the tall man with the red cloak and white wig, that, whoever he was, if the huzzaing for the Main Guard and then attacking the soldiers was the consequence of his speech to the people, that tall man is guilty in the eyes of GOD, of the murder of the five persons mentioned in the indictment, and altho' he may never be brought to a court of justice here, yet, unless he speedily flies to the city of refuge, the supreme avenger of innocent blood will surely overtake him."

However that may be, his identity has never been learned. Sam Adams evidently heard the rumors that it was he, for in one of his "Vindex" letters he defiantly challenged, "I am sollicitous that the public should know the *very man;* and the rather, because it has been impudently insinuated, that he was a gentleman *in office* in this town."

Even so direct a challenge brought forward no witnesses, and "the man in the red cloak" remains a man of mystery, striding through the crowd and disappearing into the night forever.

The little arc of soldiers was now back to the wall on the sidewalk before the Custom House, without any avenue of escape or withdrawal open to them. The crowd grew louder and more menacing minute by minute, missiles flying through the air. Pieces of ice rattled off the musket-barrels as they were parried, producing a clashing sound noted by almost all who were present. The soldiers loaded and primed their guns.

From time to time, as the crowd pressed up to the curb

and the very points of the bayonets, the soldiers would jab with their bayonet-points, shouting, "Stand off, damn you" and like warnings.

What actually touched the match to this powder keg can never be clearly known. Hugh Montgomery, the grenadier at one end of the arc of soldiers, was struck by some sort of a missile—some said a stick. It knocked his gun out of his hand, or at least he dropped it. Some witnesses said he was himself knocked down. But in any event he quickly recovered himself and immediately fired. A few seconds later, others fired also—most witnesses said seven or eight shots. Each gun was charged with two balls. Men lay still on the pavement as the smoke drifted away.

It was never possible to determine whether Captain Preston ever ordered "Fire!" or not. There was such a tumult and so many people shouted "Fire!"—whether in daring the soldiers to do so, or in crying "Where's the fire?"—that no satisfactory evidence of any command by Preston was ever found.

The blast of lead drove the people from the square. Then they returned in small parties to carry off their dead and wounded. The British squad did not interfere or fire again, but rejoined the main guard, which was in a state of alarm awaiting a general attack. It never came.

But the whole regiment was aroused and turned out under arms, forming a barrier across King Street by the Town House. A large crowd quickly gathered before it, raging with the spreading knowledge of the tragic events, rapidly getting in the mood to have it out with the soldiers then and there. Lieutenant-Governor Hutchinson appeared at this juncture about 10 P.M. and with considerable courage made an appeal to the crowd for order, promising that the soldiers would be arrested and tried for murder. Gradually the crowd dispersed, and a wholesale outpouring of blood was barely avoided. Captain Preston and his men were, true to promise, arrested that night.

The next day, a town meeting was called in Faneuil Hall, and Sam Adams made an impassioned speech demanding the withdrawal of the British troops. With John Hancock at the head of a committee, Adams marched to the Town House to see Hutchinson and Colonel Dalrymple, the British commander in Boston. When they hesitated and delayed, Adams threatened to bring fifteen thousand armed citizens to Boston to avenge the King Street deaths. As a matter of fact British intelligence had word that four thousand had actually arrived by March 8. Dalrymple, who had only about four hundred men at his command, saw the light. He promised to withdraw both regiments to Castle William in the harbor. It was done a few days later.

Despite Sam Adams' persistent efforts to get a speedy trial, delay followed delay, and the accused men were not brought to court until late November, almost nine months later. By August, British military authorities in the colonies had received assurance from England that a King's Pardon awaited any men who might be convicted, and this knowledge leaked out. Captain Preston was tried first, in late October, and was easily acquitted. Passions had cooled somewhat, the immediate cause of conflicts had been removed, tensions had subsided. In the meantime eminent lawyers had been retained for Preston and the nine soldiers. They were Josiah Quincy, Jr., and John Adams. Both incurred some unpopularity for taking the case, Quincy's own father excoriating him bitterly. It was suggested that Adams had been drawn into the case by a handsome fee, which was not true. It is odd that Sam Adams, chief opponent of the British soldiers, should have been instrumental in persuading John Adams to take the case. The best explanation is that he felt that a loyal

Whig lawyer would be less apt than a Tory lawyer to probe too deeply into local leadership that may have directly instigated the mob. All this Sam Adams, and perhaps John, too, were content to leave unexamined, on the theory that few people are bitten by letting sleeping dogs lie.

The accused faced charges that "not having the fear of God before their eyes, but being moved and seduced by the instigation of the devil and their own wicked hearts, did, on the fifth day of this instant March, at Boston aforesaid, with force and arms, feloniously, wilfully, and of their malice forethought, assault one Crispus Attucks, then and there being in the peace of God, and of the said Lord and King . . ." and so on through all the other accused and victims to make up a formidable charge of murder against each defendant.

The trial swung heavily in favor of the defendants from the very start, when the defense lawyers were able to eliminate all Bostonians as jurors, accepting only those from the surrounding territory who had not been influenced at first hand by the long series of conflicts with the troops. Not a single member of the Sons of Liberty was seated. The jury was specifically warned against the influence of widely-distributed engravings of the affair like that of Paul Revere, which showed a grinning officer waving his sword in signal to fire, with a serried row of soldiers firing a volley into a crowd engaged only in picking up the victims of what was evidently an earlier fusillade.

As a parade of witnesses told of the affair, differences in detail as to what they had observed began to develop, as is always the case in the confusion of a public tumult. But gradually the general line became clear. The crowd had assembled in a mood to seek trouble; its manner of assembly suggested strongly a prearranged plan. There were enough taunts and missiles thrown and heavy cudgels and clubs wielded to provoke the soldiers insufferably, probably even to make them fear for their lives. Captain Preston appeared most reluctant to allow an actual clash, and there was no evidence that he commanded "Fire!" He almost certainly prevented a second volley, even striking up the barrels of his soldiers' guns. And when the physician who had attended Patrick Carr, one of the victims who died ten days after the affair, testified that Carr told him the soldiers had been much provoked and that he was surprised that they did not fire much earlier than they did, the case was clearly lost. Carr was a veteran of many riots in Ireland, and told Dr. John Jeffries he had never seen soldiers bear half as much before firing. He bore no malice, he said, and was convinced that the soldier who had killed him fired only to defend himself.

John Adams, in his closing argument to the jury, summed it up in this way: ". . . . what had the soldiers to expect, when twelve persons armed with clubs, (sailors, too, between whom and soldiers there is such an antipathy, that they fight as naturally when they meet, as the elephant and the Rhinoceros) were daring enough, even at the time when they were loading their guns, to come up with their clubs and smite on their guns; what had eight soldiers to expect from such a set of people? Would it have been a prudent resolution in them, or in anybody in their situation, to have stood still, to see if the sailors would knock their brains out, or not? . . ."

The jury acquitted all but Matthew Killroy and Hugh Montgomery, who were found guilty of manslaughter and branded on the thumbs.

Such is the truth about the Boston Massacre, insofar as the agencies of human justice were able to find it at the time. The story as it has come down in history, however, began to form itself immediately thereafter. Sam Adams, under the signature of "Vindex" began writing newspaper comment on the affair, principally in the *Gazette*, which told a different story. Adams did not use the evidence as brought out at the trial, but evidence as gathered by himself and the Boston selectmen. This evidence, some ninety-six depositions, was hurriedly published in Boston (and a little later in England) as soon as possible after the affair. It was entitled *A Short Narrative of the Horrid Massacre in Boston*, etc., and it was part of a definite campaign of the Boston Whigs to use the event to rouse the spirit of independence. Copies were also sent to England in the hope of enlisting sympathy there. There are marked differences between the testimony of some of the witnesses in this book, and their testimony at the trial later the same year. Adams painted in bold strokes—blood-hungry redcoats firing wantonly into a peaceable assembly of Whigs, dogs lapping up patriot blood from the reeking pavement of King Street, Gray standing with "hands folded in his bosom" as he was brutally attacked by Killroy (whereas the trial evidence indicated that Gray was effectively wielding a cudgel). Adams slurred Carr's dying words as those of a papist who was not to be trusted. Thus the Boston Massacre of Samuel Adams became the Boston Massacre of schoolbook history.

There was no turn in this tide until about 1887, when there arose within the Massachusetts Historical Society a considerable opposition to the proposal to build a monument to the "martyrs." It was then pointed out that the inscription of "Butchers' Hall" above the Custom House in the "Revere" engraving was not exactly objective history.

But history is never finished. In 1930, 160 years after the "massacre," really new light was shed on the matter. Professor Clarence E. Carter discovered the whole file of correspondence of British Headquarters in America from 1763 to 1775. The British commandant in America at that time was General Thomas Gage. When he returned to England, he took with him his headquarters files. They were not turned over to the War Office, and Professor Carter began to suspect that they might have been preserved by the Gage heirs. And sure enough, at Firle Place, Lewes, Sussex, twelve pine chests were found, containing the whole file, undisturbed and just as Gage brought it home with him in the pine boxes. Viscount Gage, the general's descendant in occupation at Firle Place, allowed Carter to study the six thousand letters of the file, and later on they were bought by the Clements Library at Ann Arbor, Michigan, where they remain. Though Carter compiled and edited two volumes of selected correspondence between Gage and various secretaries of state in England, this great mass of correspondence is far from exhausted. It shows Gage as an able and conscientious man who, as British military commander for all North America, was virtually the King's viceroy, and was concerned with mounting problems that ranged from West Florida to Newfoundland and from New Orleans to Michigan. He was properly concerned for the welfare of his troops and well aware of the fact that they should not have been sent to Boston. In a letter to the Earl of Hillsborough, one of the King's secretaries of state, Gage referred to "an unhappy Quarrel between the People of That Town [Boston] and the soldiers," and tried to explain to an uncomprehending Hillsborough that "The Occasion which brought the Regiments to Boston, rendered them obnoxious to the people." Nevertheless, he was aware of the planning behind the disorders.

"And had the magistrates," he wrote (April 10, 1770, a month after the "massacre") and those who have Influence over the Populace in Boston, taken as much trouble to appease and restrain, as they have on too many Occasions, to inflame and excite the people to Tumults and Mischief, I am as confident, that no Blood would have been Shed in that Place. But it appears unfortunately, that their Schemes were not to be brought about through Peace and Tranquility, but by promoting Disorders. . . ."*

In short, Gage was well aware of the blind folly of ministers who, knowing nothing of America or Americans, sent troops among them in peace time. He was well aware that clashes were unavoidable and inevitable.

The Boston dock-workers and street roughs who precipitated the riot in King Street were not all of them pure patriotic idealists. Neither were the British troops entirely a set of cold-blooded, murdering ruffians. Each group was made an instrument of men higher up who made use of them at the point where the machinery of theory and policy terminates in a cutting-edge of direct action. March 5, 1770, was neither the first nor the last time in history that that was true.

The Trial of the British Soldiers, in the Superior Court of Judicature, Court of Assize, and General Gaol Delivery held in Boston during November, 1770, etc., the contemporary account of the court proceeding on which much of the foregoing is based, as well as the *Short Narrative,* are rather scarce books. If available, they are of course, indispensable contemporary sources. Sam Adams' part in the affair is discussed at length in John C. Miller's *Sam Adams, Pioneer in Propaganda* (Boston, 1936), and a selection of his newspaper pieces under the name of "Vindex" and others, is in Vol. 1 and 2 of *The Writings of Samuel Adams* (N.Y., 1904-1906), edited by Harry Alonzo Cushing. Many good illustrations of the propaganda aspect of the struggle are shown

* Clarence Carter, *The Correspondence of General Thomas Gage* (New Haven: Yale University Press, 1931). Quoted by permission of the publisher.

in *Propaganda and the American Revolution* by Philip Davidson (Chapel Hill, 1941). John Adams' part is described in John T. Morse's *John Adams* in the American Statesmen series, and Professor Carter's volumes are *The Correspondence of General Thomas Gage* (New Haven, 1931).

It is interesting to read the almost contemporary account in Mercy Warren's three-volume history (she was the sister of James Otis, a patriot who was brutally beaten by British officers in a tavern) and to contrast it with the treatment in contemporary British histories of the war—for example, *An Impartial History of the War in America* (London, 1780) where it is dismissed as "an alarming riot in Boston between the soldiers and the inhabitants," the circumstantial account being confined to a footnote. Further material from the Gage papers is presented in the most recent study, "New Light on the Boston Massacre" by Randolph G. Adams, in *Proceedings of the American Antiquarian Society* for October, 1937 (New Series, Vol. 47).

If it is desired to pursue this story and its sequels a little farther, let me suggest the story of the Battle of Lexington as told by Stewart H. Holbrook in the chapter on "The Strange 'Battle' of Lexington" in his highly readable book *Lost Men of American History* (N.Y., 1946). Holbrook reproduces four successive drawings of the Battle of Lexington which well illustrate the development of a legend during one hundred years.

All the historical books which contain no lies are extremely tedious.

—ANATOLE FRANCE: *The Crime of Sylvester Bonnard*

THE NIGHT OF FEBRUARY 14, 1493, was a terrible one in the Atlantic. Somewhere off the Azores, two tiny caravels were being tossed like corks by the raging waters. Lightning flashed and the wind whistled across the crests of ugly cross-seas. Christopher Columbus, in the *Nina*, was able to signal from time to time to Martin Pinzón in the *Pinta*, and then even that fleeting contact was lost. Each tiny ship was alone, all the more so because the flagship *Santa Maria* had been wrecked in the Caribbean and left behind, dismantled. The two remaining ships, separated and uncertain of their position, tossed by seas that seemed almost to lift them out of the water, were down to bare poles. Both had ceased to try to steer a course, all hands intent on bare survival, simply hoping against hope that, with God's help, they might ride out the storm.

Would they all be lost after all they had achieved? Would the known world never know that they had found a new and unknown world? Would Pinzón escape, perhaps, and take all the credit? Columbus had long suspected that he might try to get home first with the news. Seldom has a man been in a more desperate position than Columbus was that night, with the angry sea swirling down the deck of the tiny, staggering caravel.

The story, then, is that Columbus sat at a desk in his lurching, careening cabin, and scrawled desperately an account of the whole voyage and its epochal results. Then, as the ship's timbers creaked and strained, and the wind screamed through the flying rigging, he wrapped the parchment in a waxed cloth, tied it, and sealed it as nearly waterproof as he could, and placed it in a tight cask. Wading to the rail across the shifting and flooded deck, he threw the cask into the sea in the hope that if all were lost, including his own life, at least his King and Queen, and his two children, would know what he had done.

That Columbus did this appears to be quite true. There is some convincing evidence that it really happened, and most of the careful students of Columbus' history accept the story. It is entirely consistent with human behavior, and it is certainly the kind of episode that one likes to believe.

But what is not true is that the manuscripts were recovered from the floating cask, and are now known. Many people believe in the existence of "Columbus' Log Book" of his first voyage, and believe that the actual account which he scrawled and consigned to the sea under such dramatic circumstances exists and is known today.

But it is not so. No such cask has ever been found, and Columbus' own accounts of his voyage and discoveries (which do exist) are not the ones so dramatically cast into the tossing Atlantic.

The first popularly-read account of the incident became known when Bartolemé de las Casas' *Historia de las Indias* was discovered in manuscript in a Madrid museum in 1875. It was immediately published in Spanish and then translated into English and published in that language. Within a very few weeks after the American edition of this history appeared, what was alleged to be the original document turned up in San Francisco, where it was offered to handwriting experts for examination. But they quickly declared that the document shown them could not possibly be more than 30 years old. It found a ready buyer, nevertheless. Soon afterward another such manuscript (or perhaps the same one) turned up in Mexico City. It had been soaked in salt water, it was damaged and torn, and bits of shell and sand adhered to its pages. None the less, the writing was quite clear, and this writing was all in German, with a lame explanation that Columbus had used that language to hide his observations from his associates.

Countless versions of the "Columbus Log" have been exhibited as the original. In 1890, for instance, a London publisher received such a manuscript from a sailor in Wales. It had been found in a box hauled up out of the sea while trawling, according to the sailor's story. This one had the appropriate barnacles and seashells carefully glued to it, but unfortunately it was found to have been *lithographed* on vellum. It was written in synthetic Elizabethan English and titled "My secrete Log Boke." Several copies of this fakery had been produced, evidently in anticipation of the World's Columbian Exposition planned for Chicago in 1893.

Every few years another candidate turns up. Not a single one has ever passed the critical scrutiny of the scholars.

The plain fact seems to be that if Columbus really made this dramatic gesture in the face of destiny, the cask and the manuscript have never been found. And since more than 450 years have passed, it has become highly unlikely that it ever will be. And yet, who knows? The ways of fate and truth are very strange, and there may yet be lying, cast up upon the rocks on some remote coast, a battered wooden cask containing this precious "Log Book" of Columbus.

Those who wish to know what Columbus *did* write may find a beautiful facsimile of the original printing with a translation of his first letter announcing his discovery, printed by the Lenox Library (now the New York Public Library) which has a copy of the original edition. Bartolemé de las Casas and Martin Fernandez de Navarette published summaries of Columbus' diaries, which are all we have, since the originals here again have been lost. And, of course, the excellent biographies of Columbus by Salvador de Madariaga and Samuel Eliot Morison have absorbing discussions of the whole matter. New York University published (1939) *The Case of the Columbus Letter*, an absorbing account of certain disputed Columbus letters and material. An excellent selection of Columbus' writings about his discoveries, with a critical discussion of the various manuscripts and early editions, is in *Select Letters of Christopher Columbus*, published by the Hakluyt Society of London in 1870, and translated and edited by R. H. Major.

So very difficult a matter it is to trace and find out the truth of anything by history.

—PLUTARCH: *Lives*

George Washington's Cherry Tree

THERE WAS A TIME, NOT SO long ago, when even those who knew nothing else about George Washington knew that as a boy he cut down a cherry tree and, on being questioned about it, replied, "Father, I cannot tell a lie. I did it with my little hatchet."

Today, the story has been exploded so many times that it is not quite so universally believed. Yet one feels that it is dying out, not so much because there is so little reason to believe it, as because the fashion for such primly-perfect little boys has passed. However, the story of how the little myth arose remains an interesting one, in itself well worth retelling.

When George Washington died, on the 14th of December of the last year of the eighteenth century, there was instantly a great demand for the story of his life. The demand was catered to by the immediate publication of many little biographies in book form, most of them somewhat less accurate and complete than would be the obituary of such a man in a modern newspaper. Within ten weeks more than four hundred "mortuary sermons" were printed, which were in effect short biographies.

One of the biographies which appeared during the year (1800) following Washington's death was by Mason Locke Weems, known as "Parson Weems."

Weems was a parson, right enough, a regularly-ordained Episcopal minister. He called himself "a former rector of Mt. Vernon Parish." There never was any "Mt. Vernon Parish." Mt. Vernon was in Truro Parish. Weems had no better right to the title he took than that he had occasionally preached at Pohick Church, where Washington often attended. But Weems was a real enthusiast for books. As one of the earliest American "traveling salesmen" in the book business, he sold them all along the Eastern Seaboard. He knew the book market, and he knew what the American people liked. Even before Washington died, he was preparing a biography for the market he knew would immediately arise.

In June, 1799, about six months before Washington's death, Weems wrote: "I have nearly ready for the press a piece christened, or to be christened, 'The Beauties of Washington.' 'Tis artfully drawn up, enlivened with anecdotes, and in my humble opinion marvelously fitted, *'ad capitandum gustom populi Americani!'* "

And when Washington had died (December 14, 1799) Weems wrote almost immediately thereafter (on January 12, 1800) to Matthew Carey, his publisher, as follows:

"Washington you know is gone! Millions are gaping to read something about him. I am very nearly primed and cocked for 'em. 6 months ago I got myself to collect anecdotes of him. You know I live conveniently for that work. My plan! I give his history sufficiently minute—I accompany him from his start, thro the French & Indian & British or Revolutionary wars, to the president's chair, to the throne in the hearts of 5,000,000 people. I then go on to show that his unparalleled rise and elevation were owing to his Great Virtues. . . . Thus I hold up his great Virtues to the imitation of Our Youth. All this I have lined and enlivened with Anecdotes apropos interesting and Entertaining."

The Weems' *Washington* sold like hot cakes. "Washington outsells anything I have, no comparison," he wrote to Carey. Edition followed edition (and does, to this day). Gradually Weems expanded his story, continuing to "enliven" it with further anecdotes. In the edition of 1806 there first appeared the immortal yarn about the cherry tree. Because few people today know exactly how Weems told it, I reproduce it here:

"The following anecdote," he wrote, "is a *case in point*. It is too valuable to be lost, and too true to be doubted; for it was communicated to me by the same excellent lady to whom I am indebted for the last.

" 'When George,' said she, 'was about six years old, he was made the wealthy master of a *hatchet!* of which, like most little boys, he was immoderately fond; and was constantly going about chopping everything that came in his way. One day, in the garden, where he often amused himself hacking his mother's pea-sticks, he unluckily tried the edge of his hatchet on the body of a beautiful young English cherry-tree, which he barked so terribly that I don't believe the tree ever got the better of it. The next morning the old gentleman, finding out what had befallen his tree, which, by the way, was a great favourite, came into the house, and with much warmth asked for the mischievous author, declaring at the same time that he would not have taken five guineas for his tree. Nobody could tell him anything about it. Presently George and his hatchet made their appearance. 'George,' said his father, 'do you know who killed that beautiful little cherry tree yonder in the garden?' This was a *tough question*, and George staggered under it for a moment, but quickly recovered himself: and looking at his father, with the sweet face of youth brightened with the inexpressible charm of all-conquering truth, he bravely cried out, 'I can't tell a lie, Pa; you know I can't tell a lie. I did cut it with my hatchet.' 'Run to my arms, you dearest boy,' cried his father in transports, 'run to my arms; glad am I, George, that you killed my tree, for you have paid me for it a thousand fold. Such an act of heroism in my son is more worth than a thousand trees, though blossomed with silver, and their fruits of purest gold."

Whether the young Washington or his father appears more utterly unreal in this obviously fabricated incident is a "tough question." As a matter of fact, it has been found that Weems probably got the idea from a quite similar incident which happened to him and one of his own children.

Weems is also responsible for the story that Washington threw a stone (later elaborations claim it was a dollar) across the Rappahannock. Here is Weems' story:

"Col. Lewis Willis, his playmate and kinsman, has been heard to say that he has often seen him throw a stone across the Rappahannock, at the lower ferry at Fredericksburg. It would be no easy matter to find a man, nowadays, who could do it." (However that may be, it was not hard to find one in the Nineteen-twenties. Walter Johnson, the baseball pitcher, did it easily.)

This story might even be true, and it is unfortunate that we are forced to depend on Weems, who is so generally unreliable. The best we can say is that we do not actually know whether it is true or not. It is most unlikely that it was a dollar, for everything else we know of Washington argues that it would have been most unlike him to throw away a Spanish dollar, then worth five or six shillings, and important money in that day. Washington was neither careless or profligate with money. But the stone—it is possible. All we can say is that it is tradition, unsupported by evidence. We do know on the best evidence that Washington had a strong, muscular physique, that he was among the most graceful and finest horsemen of a day when riding was important, that he wrestled and climbed, and that his physical endurance was phenomenal. But the facts speak for themselves and need no elaboration from fanciful tradition.

There are plenty of people who feel that there is no harm in such bits of sugar-icing on the cake of history—certainly Parson Weems does not seem to have done any harm to millions of American children who read his yarns (almost surely including Abraham Lincoln). But to others, distortion and untruth are distortion and untruth, however noble their purpose. And for those who really want to know the Father of their Country, the ascertained facts and the plain truth are quite inspiring enough.

For further study of this matter, turn, of course, first to Weems' book itself and make your own estimate of its general trustworthiness. Weems wrote other biographies, like those of Marion and Penn, but even a hundred years ago Evert Duyckinck, who with his brother George Long Duyckinck, wrote the *Cyclopedia of American Literature*, dryly characterized Weems as "the biographer of many heroes, in whose hands the trumpet of fame never sounded an uncertain blast." Weems himself has been interestingly written about by Lawrence Wroth (*Parson Weems*) and by Emily Ellsworth Ford Skeel (*Mason Locke Weems, His Works and Ways*). On Washington himself, Douglas Southall Freeman's six-volume biography is the last word, or try Stephenson and Dunn's, in two volumes. And if you want to live with Washington at Mt. Vernon and know him as a human being, read his *Diaries*, edited by John C. Fitzpatrick. One of the newer books to treat of the cherry-tree legend is *Parson Weems of the Cherry Tree* by Harold Kellock (N. Y., 1928).

The "Donation of Constantine"

THE STUBBORN PERSISTENCE OF error is well shown by the fact that five hundred years have passed since the *Donation of Constantine* was shown to be a forgery. Yet today many people believe that the great Emperor Constantine, grateful for his conversion to Christianity and perhaps also for having been healed of leprosy by Pope Sylvester, granted to that pope and his successors not only spiritual supremacy over all other patriarchates, but also temporal dominion over Rome, Italy, and all that vast territory now known vaguely as "the West."

This controversy concerned itself only with the temporal power of the Popes. The Church of Rome has, of course, never placed any reliance for its claims of spiritual superiority on any grant from Constantine or any other temporal ruler. These claims are based on other foundations. But the confused question of the temporal authority of the Popes has long been interwoven with the controversy over the *Donation*, a strange document produced some time during the eighth century, more than four hundred years after the death of Constantine in 337.

Real temporal power in the West had long passed from

29

the Romans into the hands of Christianized tribes in the north of Europe, and the vast empire of the Franks dominated all of what is now France, the Low Countries, Germany and Austria. The great Charlemagne was at its head. He was the closest friend and ally of Pope Adrian I, who regarded the Frankish power as the protector of the Holy See and all its possessions. But Pope Adrian was ambitious not merely to hold the territories he ruled by virtue of Charlemagne's protection, but to gain more. He approached Charlemagne about 775 with the argument that while the Emperor had done well in affirming his rights to small territories in Italy and defending Pope Adrian against Lombard princes who threatened them, this was really only a small installment on what was literally due the Holy See by virtue of the *Donation of Constantine*, and that Charlemagne was to regard himself as successor and executor of the will of the first great Christian emperor, with obligations unfulfilled until the actual territory controlled by the Pope should comprise all that vague domain known as "the West."

It is not now thought likely that Pope Adrian confronted Charlemagne with the actual document by which Constantine had so munificently endowed the Papacy. That was to come later. The demand for such a document as visual evidence of the Papal claims was obvious. And unfortunately history is full of examples in which a document badly needed is inevitably produced. This one was produced sometime during the eighth century. Exactly by whom it was written is still the subject of very animated research.

Indeed, very little use appears to have been made of the document during the ninth and tenth centuries, but about that time, when an aura of venerability had gathered about it, increasing reference to it began to appear. From the twelfth century on, it became a powerful weapon in the struggle between temporal and spiritual power in Europe.

Both the friends and the enemies of the claims of the Papacy to temporal power during the Middle Ages generally regarded the document as quite genuine, though even in the tenth century the first doubts had been cast upon its genuineness by Leo of Vercelli, chancellor to the Emperor Otto III, who rejected its claims. Few even among the supporters of the Empire as against the temporal claims of the Papacy, doubted it, however they might cry out against it as the *fons et origo malorum* (the very fountainhead and source of all evils), and berate the memory of Constantine as one who had betrayed the trust that had been placed in him as temporal Emperor.

Indeed, in the ninth century the *Donation* was already included in the collection of documents known as the *False Decretals*, which included many other papers later shown to be forgeries, and whose authorship has never been determined. These tended to show older precedents than had been known for the supreme authority of the Pope over the provincial synods, and here again it seems fairly clear that someone had gone to work to provide documents which would be useful in backing up claims. The most exacting scholarship has failed to determine precisely by whom, when, or where, the *False Decretals* were written—the best that scholarship has been able to do is to determine that they were not written at Rome, but probably at Metz, between 829 and 840. Pope Nicholas I was the first to accept them as genuine, to promulgate them, and to use them as a basis for claims to spiritual authority, especially as against Hincmar, Archbishop of Rheims, who had grown so powerful politically as to flout, in certain matters, the Roman authority.

The first scholarly and definitive refutation of the genuineness of the *Donation* was not made until 1440. Laurentius (or Lorenzo) Valla was a Roman critic and scholar who had delved deeply into the Latin language and written much about its usage. He was one of the group of scholars who were rising in Italy and whose studies were later to be called The Revival of Learning, one of the characteristic features of the Renaissance. This turning back to the study of the Latin classics nursed the genius of men like Dante and Petrarch and Boccaccio, Poggio and Machiavelli and Valla himself. Because it turned away from medieval study of scholastic theology and philosophy to the study of man and his works and thoughts, it was sometimes called "Humanism."

Applying to the text of the *False Decretals* and the *Donation* the principles they had developed for critical study of ancient manuscripts, Valla proved the *Donation* a complete falsification, and utterly destroyed many of the documents included in the *False Decretals*. It was a daring act, for Valla was flying at once in the face of established tradition and ecclesiastical authority. But Valla was the private secretary of Alphonso V of Aragon and had his patron's protection in the controversy which inevitably followed his skepticism. Valla was summoned before an inquisitorial tribunal, but escaped when Alphonso intervened in his favor. In later years Valla was not only reconciled to the Church, but was actually made Apostolic Secretary by Pope Nicholas V. Thus the exposure of one of history's great falsifications became the happy occasion for the earliest reconciliation between the rising tide of Humanism and the ecclesiastical authority.

The fraudulence of the *Donation* is now universally conceded, though controversy over it continued until well toward the end of the eighteenth century. Later studies have largely been engaged in trying to find out precisely where and by whom the document was actually written. It has been argued that it was produced by the Franks in an effort to legitimize the reign of Charlemagne and thus justify the driving of the Greeks from Italy. Or was it the work of some over-zealous Papal clerk in the time of Adrian I, intent on legitimizing the territorial dominion which the Pope had succeeded in setting up in Italy?

Whoever wrote it, and for whatever purpose, scholars are now agreed that the *Donation* is a barefaced forgery. And yet, for several hundred years it was a powerful weapon in the hands of the political powers of Europe. Popes Sylvester II and Gregory V appealed to it in support of territorial claims, and in 1050 Pope Leo IX did the same in a controversy with Byzantium. Gibbon says that in his day it was "among the decrees of canon law." For two hundred years even the opponents who railed at it so bitterly never thought to challenge its authority. But, of course, neither the techniques for judging the authenticity of such a document, nor indeed, even the critical spirit which might have questioned it, were yet in existence.

And so a thousand years passed before a document concocted in A.D. 750-800 was definitely shown to be one of the great historical impositions of all time.

The most amusing, if not the most accurate account of the *Donation* is in Gibbon's *The History of the Decline and Fall of the Roman Empire*. Unfortunately it is in precisely such a matter that Gibbon is at his weakest, because of his pronounced anti-Church inclinations. The *Encyclopaedia Britannica* (14th Edition) has a balanced article, and the *Cambridge Medieval History* has a good discussion. It happens that most of the critically scholarly studies are in German and hence are not readily available to the average reader. But Richard Winston's *Charlemagne* (Indianapolis, 1954), one of the newer studies, suffers from neither of those handicaps.

The Mecklenberg, N.C., Declaration of Independence

PEOPLE, BEING HUMAN, ARE avid to believe anything that reflects credit upon themselves. The citizen of a country likes to believe that his country's motives are pure, its statesmen honorable, its soldiers brave, its scientists effective (and first with the important inventions). This applies equally to one's own state or county. Most people like to think they live in the best city, and family history and ancestry that seem to reflect credit on present bearers of the name are readily credited. It is so easy to believe good of oneself.

Thus history is full of eager partisans and supporters of one story or another which reflects credit on their country, their race, their community, their family.

One of the most stirring events in American history is, of course, the Declaration of Independence at Philadelphia, and we still celebrate the anniversary of its date, July 4, 1776. (By the way, most people imagine the delegates sitting about and signing the Continental Congress' Declaration on the day it was adopted, whereas the official parchment copy so reverently preserved in Washington was not actually engrossed and signed until August 2, and by some delegates even later.) Note, also, that Richard Henry Lee had submitted a resolution to the Congress on June 7, which declared independence, and this was adopted on July 2. Thus we might well celebrate Independence Day on July 2. But in the meantime, on June 10, a committee had been appointed to draw up a "declaration" in support of the resolution, and this, drafted largely by Jefferson and adopted on July 4, is the public "declaration" which has become official, rather than the "resolution" of two days earlier. Note the date June 7, however, for it was on that day that independence was formally proposed and began its course through the regular legislative channels.

Now there has never been any question that this resolution and this declaration were the real and effective ones from which stemmed an independent United States. But on April 30, 1819, the *Raleigh Register* came out with a story to the effect that on May 20, 1775, a meeting of citizens of Mecklenburg, N. C. (the county in the western part of the state around Charlotte) had adopted a declaration of independence in which the participants declared that "a free and independent people are, and of right ought to be, a sovereign and self-governing association under the control of no other power than that of our God and the General Government of Congress." The newspaper account admitted that the original document could not be produced, having been destroyed by fire in 1800, but based the account on the recollections of certain very old men, whose local reputation was (and is) excellent.

Such a date is a full year ahead of the national declaration, and further, there is a similarity of language that suggested that the later national declaration had drawn heavily on the previous one at Mecklenburg.

The *Raleigh Register* story was soon reprinted by the *Essex Register* in Massachusetts, and there John Adams read it. He immediately sat down and wrote a rather short-tempered note to Jefferson, asking why he had not been informed of the Mecklenburg action at the time, noting that he could have used it in persuading recalcitrants to go along with independence. This added to Jefferson's annoyance at the suggestion of plagiarism on his part, and he returned a letter in the same key to Adams: ". . . . I believe it spurious," he wrote. "I deem it to be a very unjustifiable quiz, like that of the volcano, so minutely related to us as having broken out in North Carolina, some half-dozen years ago, in that part of the country, and perhaps in that very county of Mecklenburg, for I do not remember its precise locality. . . ."

Jefferson went on to point out that it would have been most singular for such an incident to have escaped notice at the time, for ". . . would not every advocate of independence have rung the glories of Mecklenburg County of North Carolina in the ears of the doubting Dickinson and others, who hung so heavily on us? . . ."

It is indeed strange that so ringing a declaration, if made, should have been ignored at the time and for forty-five years thereafter.

Nevertheless the declaration was generally accepted from 1819 until 1847. At this time an authentic copy of the *S. Carolina Gazette* of June 16, 1775, was unearthed in England. This copy described a meeting at Charlotte on May 31, 1775 (*not* May 20) in which certain resolutions were adopted. But these were not quite so uncompromising a declaration of independence as had been reported, and they did not quite so closely foreshadow the language of the national declaration of July 4, 1776.

The matter is still controversial, but what seems most likely is this. Old men, recalling that there had been a meeting at Charlotte concerned with independence, confused the date, setting it on May 20 rather than May 31. They then quite honestly tried to reconstruct the language, there being no written record, and they were perhaps unconsciously influenced by the ringing language of the Philadelphia declaration, and so came to attribute some of it to Mecklenburg. The meeting of the thirty-first is well authenticated. Were there two meetings? The known language adopted on the thirty-first is not that of a real Declaration of Independence. Was there a previous meeting, at which language very similar to that of the later Philadelphia declaration was adopted? Or did the memory of old men, stimulated by local pride, enhance the whole affair into a real declaration of independence antedating by a full year the one we celebrate? The general weight of scholarship says they did, and that the uncompromising declaration of May 20 was never made at a meeting that never took place.

But the State of North Carolina says yes. It placed the date May 20, 1775, on the state flag and on the state seal. The legislature declared May 20 a holiday. At one time, it was compulsory for the state's public schools to teach the May 20 declaration. The Centennial was solemnly celebrated in 1875.

The whole matter has been complicated by at least one attempt to authenticate the Mecklenburg Declaration, which proved to be a sheer fake. In 1905 *Collier's Magazine* published a facsimile of the first page of *The Cape Fear Mercury* for June 3, 1775. This contained a full text of the "declaration" of May 20. Critics showed that unfortunately June 3, 1775, had not been a Friday as the paper indicated, that the type did not correspond to that used in known copies of the *Mercury*, and that the paper had suspended publication before the date of the copy that had been reproduced.

All of which does not preclude the possibility that some day evidence may be found that will prove the May 20 declaration to have been just what its supporters have believed. All that can be said is that up to now the majority of those who have studied the question agree that the May 20, 1775, meeting with its unequivocal declaration in Jeffersonian terms cannot be shown to have happened at all.

Unless the May 20 meeting should sometime be shown to have adopted a declaration of independence in really uncompromising terms, it would, even if such a meeting was held, be less important than, for example, the resolutions adopted even earlier, September 9, 1774, at Suffolk, Massachusetts. These were almost as militant and suggestive of independence as the ones known to have been adopted in Mecklenburg on May 31, 1775.

As a matter of fact, with the spirit of independence cropping out here and there throughout the colonies, it is quite possible that many local resolutions looking to independence were passed in various places, like those in Mendon, Massachusetts, in 1773. But even then they would be local, and nothing more than straws pointing toward the great event which took place in Philadelphia in July, 1776.

The reader who has a special interest in any of the states which were colonies in the 1770's might wish to pursue the question of early meetings in his state looking toward independence. It is always possible that new material will be found in this field. The most detailed discussions of the Mecklenburg Declaration are in scholarly journals like that of J. C. Welling in the *North American Review*, April, 1874. See also William Henry Hoyt's *The Mecklenburg Declaration of Independence*, (N.Y., 1907). Hoyt began his researches with the intention of defending the local tradition, but became convinced as he went deeper into the matter that it did not happen, refuting in detail the book of two years before of the same title, by George W. Graham (N.Y. and Washington, 1905), who essayed to prove the validity of the meeting of May 20. There is a good general discussion of the problem in Appendix 2, Vol. 3, pp. 570-582 of the *Life of Thomas Jefferson*, by Henry S. Randall, (N.Y., 1858).

History ceases to be a series of objective events in regular progression, whether that progression be intelligible and capable of a clear and comprehensible description or not, and becomes dependent on the cast of a mind of a particular human being who selects from the mass of recorded material what suits his interests, gratifies his feelings, and falls in with his peculiar aspirations; its arrangement depends on his understanding, and its form on his artistic ability.

—MAX NORDAU: *The Interpretation of History*

The Protocols of the Elders of Zion

To THOSE WHO THINK OF HIS-
torical error as mere comedy (as it may be) or as a game
played by pedantic scholars (which it can become), let us
present the tragedy of the *Protocols of the Elders of Zion*.
The lives of thousands of innocents may have been sacrificed
to this historical monstrosity; hatred and suffering and tears
have been its fruit for fifty years.

The people of this world act, not necessarily on what is the
truth, but necessarily on what they believe to be the truth.
The anti-Semitic activities which have stained the past hundred years with blood and tears stem, of course, from a
body of anti-Semitic belief. We are concerned here with one
instance in which the authority and respectability of history
was used to re-enforce such beliefs. The manner of this be-
trayal and misuse of history was as follows:

In the year of 1905, a year in which Russia was swept by
tides of upheaval, revolutionary restlessness and fear, there
appeared from the presses of Tsarskoe Selo a publication
called *The Great in the Little* (*Velikoe v Malom*). Its sponsor was Sergei Nilus, a religious mystic greatly agitated by his
belief in the imminent appearance of the Antichrist. In an

40

appendix to this work there was presented an alleged account of secret sessions of the First Zionist Congress, held in 1897 at Basle. There were twenty-four "Protocols" listed, which it was claimed were read to the "Elders" or "Wise Men" of Zion as a plan for future action by Jewish leaders to enslave the world. By violence, by terror, by exploiting the baser instincts of the *Goyim*, or gentiles, by the power of gold and the influence of liberalism, including that of Freemasonry, by using the press to confuse and the constitutions to enfeeble the existing states, by appeals to materialism, international hatreds and wars, a new world-wide state was to arise ruled by a Jewish master operating through malleable Gentile "stooges."

No original documents or photographic reproductions of such documents were offered. In fact Nilus wrote that the documents themselves had been copied by his agents. There were no signatures—nothing but the printed version of an alleged copy.

Next, one G. Butni, a violent anti-Semite and a founder of the Russian Black Hundreds, issued a book at St. Petersburg in 1906, called *The Enemies of the Human Race*, in which a somewhat enlarged version of these same protocols was offered.

To these two versions, largely to that of Nilus, thousands, perhaps millions of reprints owe their origin. They not only swept Russia, but went into French and English versions, as well as Polish, Finnish, Japanese, Chinese and Arabic. Alfred Rosenberg launched them in 1923 in a Germany not yet Nazi, as part of Hitler's campaign to take power. Swiss and South African Nazi-type politicians issued the material, and in America Henry Ford's *Dearborn Independent* ran From May 22 to October 2, 1920, a series called "The International Jew" largely based on them. Ford did not actually publish the text of the *Protocols*, but the parallels were too clear to be questioned. As late as 1938 in the United States, Father Charles Coughlin republished similar material in *Social Justice*. And it seems likely that even today the *Protocols* are being reissued by those who think they can use them in their business.

Yet these "documents" roused the suspicion of the critical-minded from the moment they first appeared, and never since 1921 has there been any doubt in the mind of any impartial student that the whole thing was a malicious concoction and a monstrous forgery.

For instance, neither Nilus nor Butni was ever able to give a satisfactory or even a consistent account of how they got their copies of the documents. At various times they described them as stolen from a Masonic lodge or sneaked from the rooms of Theodor Herzl, the Jewish Zionist leader who had presided at the 1897 meetings. There were references in the report of the proceedings of the 1897 meeting to events which did not take place until 1899. There were statements insulting to the intelligence of the allegedly wise elders, like the ridiculous one that Jews had fomented and led the French Revolution. And so on. Enough to make the cautious and the critical back away from the story.

Then, in 1921, a *London Times* correspondent in Constantinople, one Philip Graves, bought an old book from a refugee Russian who had once been a member of the Czarist secret police. He bought the book idly, merely as a favor to help an acquaintance in distress, but as he thumbed through it, phrases, sentences, paragraphs, began to sound familiar. Suddenly he realized that here were whole passages of the exact language of the *Protocols*, which he had read a short time before.

The book had lost its title-page, and Graves sent it to the British Museum for identification. It turned out to be *Dialogue in Hell Between Machiavelli and Montesquieu* published in Paris in 1865 by Maurice Joly. It was a satire on the rule of Napoleon III, of sufficient pungency to get M. Joly fined and jailed by the authorities.

The parallels of language were deadly, and definitely showed plagiarism. But was it not possible that the Jewish Elders themselves had stolen the language of M. Joly? Technically possible, and chronologically possible, yes. But likely, no.

In that same year, 1921, a committee of New York Jews proved that General P. T. Rachkovski, a Russian secret agent in Paris, had woven together the material taken from M. Joly's *Dialogues*. This evidence, with more that had been found out in the meantime, was presented to a Swiss Court in 1934-35 when a group of Swiss Jews sued Theodor Fischer and other extreme Swiss Nationalists for circulating literature which included the *Protocols*. The case at issue was merely whether the publication fell within certain Swiss laws against improper literature. But in the course of the trial, the whole evidence against the genuineness of the *Protocols* was reviewed without challenge by the defendants. It was shown that the documents were evidently prepared by the secret police to influence the Czar, who originally accepted them, but must have been shown their falsity, as they were not produced in subsequent state trials in Russia in which they would have been most useful if genuine. The Swiss court's verdict, May 14, 1935, was that the documents were "a forgery, a plagiarism, and silly nonsense."

Even before this, however, Henry Ford had been forced to retract his "International Jew" series, specifically repudiating the *Protocols* as a basis for it. The series proper had been ended in late 1920, but in 1924 it was revived, and made reference to one Aaron Sapiro, a Chicago lawyer and organizer for certain farm cooperatives, as principal in a Jewish plot to control agriculture. Sapiro sued for a million dollars in damages, and the suit came to trial in U. S. District Court, Detroit, in March, 1927. In the meantime, Ford's new Model A car was about to come out, and he could not forget the mounting near-boycott which had followed his publications in 1920. On July 7, 1927, Ford had had enough. To the surprise of all, including his own lawyers, a statement suddenly appeared in the newspapers, containing an apology by Ford which paved the way to settlement. What we are concerned with here is that the *Protocols* were specifically repudiated in the statement:

". . . I confess I am deeply mortified," wrote Ford, "that this journal (*The Independent*), which is intended to be constructive and not destructive, has been made the medium for resurrecting exploded fictions, for giving currency to the so-called protocols of the wise men of Zion which have been demonstrated, as I learn, to be gross forgeries. . . ."

Ford insisted that he had never read, and did not know what had been published in his paper, and an editorial employee, William Cameron, had already publicly assumed all the responsibility. Remaining copies of the printed material, together with masses of "evidence" that had been gathered by Ford detectives during the *Independent*'s campaign, were destroyed. But unfortunately, much of the harm done was beyond recall, for the pamphlets and articles under the Ford name had already been widely distributed in Europe, especially by the publicity experts who were well on the way to putting over a rising young anti-Semite named Adolf Hitler. To them the *Protocols* were a mine all the easier exploited when they could be presented in connection with the great American God of Efficiency.

One additional touch was added when it was found that Nilus, in later editions, added material lifted from a novel, *Biarritz*, by Herman Josedsche (1868), a chapter of which was called "In the Jewish Cemetery of Prague."

Yet all this did not stay the hand of Father Coughlin even ten years after Ford's public retraction.

Nor can one hope that this whole monstrous inspired fabrication will not reappear. The mere fact that the most careful investigation has shown it to be entirely false will probably not prevent the unscrupulous from trotting it out again for their own evil purposes. All we can do here is to drive one more nail in the lid of its coffin, hoping that, with enough nails, the lid will eventually hold.

Any one of a dozen good studies of anti-Semitism provides a clear account of the *Protocols*. Graves wrote a book about his discoveries. The best summary of the evidence is in *An Appraisal of the Protocols of Zion* by John S. Curtiss (Columbia University Press, 1942). Curtiss takes pains to point out that he is a New England Yankee from away back, and hence devoid of the sort of personal bias in the matter that may have affected several previous and even more detailed accounts. His summary is signed by thirteen of the best-known historians in the United States, attesting it to be a sound study and convincing to the signers that the infamous *Protocols* are a shameless fraud.

One of the first duties of man is not to be duped, to be aware of his world; and to derive the significance of human experience from events that never occurred is surely an enterprise of doubtful value.

—CARL BECKER: *Everyman His Own Historian*

Pocohantas and John Smith

ONE OF THE FAVORITE STORIES of American history is the one about Pocahontas and John Smith—how the bold English captain was taken by savages in Virginia—how he was condemned by stern Powhatan to die—how the clubs were poised over his head to beat out his life—how the beautiful Indian Princess threw her arms about his neck, ready to die with him—how Powhatan, stirred by his daughter's devotion, relented, and Smith was saved.

The story has everything: the bravely-whiskered captain, the barbarian Indian "Emperor's Court," the beautiful thirteen-year-old Princess interposing her love to fend off death, Smith's release, and the happy ending—how the Princess married an Englishman and became the charmer of London society. Yes, the story has everything.

It entered readily into the folklore of a country eager to create its own traditions. In the time of Jefferson, the leading hotel in Washington was the Indian Queen, and its large swinging sign displayed to all who passed in Pennsylvania Avenue a gay figure of Pocahontas. She was a theme for the carvers of ship's figureheads, and Antonio Capellano carved over the west door of the Rotunda in the Capitol at Washing-

46

ton a frieze depicting in marble the romantic incident. Several early American plays were written around the theme, and eager youngsters learned the story from Peter Parley's *Stories About Captain John Smith* (1829) which rhapsodized "What a worthy girl this was! She was a savage, but her deed was noble!" John Esten Cooke, the Virginia novelist, went so far as to suggest that Miranda in Shakespeare's *The Tempest* is a reflection of Pocahontas. Yes, the story has everything—everything, that is, except a good, substantial backing in sound evidence.

Yet it may all be quite true. After three hundred and fifty years, all that can be said is that it stands alone on Smith's personal say-so, and that is known to be rather unstable ground. The lack of confirmatory evidence has led many students to conclude that the whole story is nothing but romantic embellishment by Smith, though it is only fair to say that there are a few who stoutly stand their ground and maintain its literal truth. Let us follow this saga as it insinuates itself into history.

In 1607, James Towne was a spattering of rude huts around a miniature fort, and its settlers were having rough going. Most of them were ill-equipped and ill-qualified for the adventure. But not Captain John Smith. He was only about twenty-eight years old, but he had already had enough adventures to fill a book before sailing for Virginia at all. He had been a cavalry soldier in the Netherlands, a pirate (or privateer, there having been in those days often not much difference), had done great single-handed deeds of arms in a Turkish campaign for Sigismund, King of Hungary. He was then captured, sold into slavery, and escaped, "befriended by a Turkish lady of quality." So he told it, and Thomas Fuller, contemporary author of a series of brief biographies, including the first one ever written of Smith, commented wryly that Smith's story was adorned "with many strange performances, the scene whereof is laid at such a distance, they are cheaper credited than confuted."

There is, however, no doubt at all that Smith had outstanding personal courage, intrepidity, and administrative ability. The London Company, which had invested several million dollars in its Virginia "plantation," is not likely to have entrusted its venture to the command of a windy braggart. The company must first have been well satisfied, after investigation, of Smith's sound qualities. No one questions today that, though Smith is the hero of Smith's writings, his courage and military discipline were major factors in holding the tiny colony together. But mingled with all his golden qualities there was also a high admixture of brass.

In the winter days, then, of late December, 1607, Smith took two men and trekked inland up the Chickahominy River to trade with the Indians for badly needed corn, and probably in the ever-present hope of finding gold or a water connection with the Great South Sea. The party ran into hostile Indians. There was a fight; Smith's companions were killed; he was captured. After some days, his captor, Powhatan, sent him back to Jamestown.

These bare facts are known, not only from Smith but from others of the colony. The details of the Pocahontas affair are necessarily those of Smith alone. This is unfortunate for, as Fuller put it in his *The Worthies of England*, "his perils, preservations, dangers, deliverances, they seem to most men above belief, to some beyond truth. Yet we have two witnesses to attest them, the prose and the pictures, both in his own book, and it soundeth much to the diminution of his deeds, that he alone is the herald to publish and proclaim them."

Smith first published and proclaimed them in London in 1608, the year after they occurred. Written within a few months of the events, the account was sent to London and issued under the title, *A True Relation of Such Occurrences of Noate as Hath Happened in Virginia.* This earliest account of Smith himself tells of the capture, and says that Powhatan welcomed him "with good wordes, and great Platters of sundrie Victuals, assuring mee his friendship, and my libertie within four dayes." Smith specifically notes that when he was sent back to Jamestown, it was with an escort of four men.

But in this first account, there is no mention of Pocahontas at all, let alone any account of her dramatic intercession for Smith's life.

On Smith's return to Jamestown, he was arrested for having permitted the loss of the lives of his two companions, and was apparently in some danger of being hanged. But the timely arrival of a ship with new colonists created a diversion and saved him. It seems clearly due to his energy and ability during the following year that the colony was able to survive at all. In 1609, Smith was badly injured by the explosion of a bag of gunpowder and left the colony for England, never to return. It is significant that the days of worst suffering, the "starving time," followed his departure.

Thus Smith was in England when in 1613 Pocahontas was betrayed into the hands of the English by a bribed chieftain, and was held at Jamestown as a hostage for certain English captives. Long before that she had become well known as a child to the colonists through frequent visits to the fort. In April, 1614, she married John Rolfe, one of the more prosperous of the settlers, becoming the second of his three wives. Rolfe was the first to initiate in Virginia the systematic growing and curing of tobacco for export.

Smith severed his connection with the London Company, and took service with the Virginia Company, for whom he made several exploring voyages to New England. In fact, he offered in 1619 to pilot the Pilgrim Fathers to America, but his offer was not accepted.

Smith wrote a great deal during these later years. He made the first accurate map of the New England coast from the Penobscot to Cape Cod, and the very names "New England" and "Plymouth" may be of his designing. In 1624, he published in London *The General History of Virginia, New England, and the Summer Isles*, and in this history there appeared for the first time the story of Pocahontas. And this is how he told it:

"At this entrance before the King, all the people gave a great shout. The Queene of *Appamatuck* was appointed to bring him water to wash his hands, and another brought him a bunch of feathers in stead of a Towell to dry them: having feasted him after their best barbarous manner they could, a long consultation was held, but the conclusion was, two great stones were brought before *Powhatan:* then as many as could layd hands on him, dragged him to them, and thereon laid his head, and being ready with their clubs, to beate out his braines, *Pocahontas* the kings dearest daughter, when no intreaty could prevaile, got his head in her armes, and laid her owne upon his to save him from death: whereat the Emperor was contented he should live to make him hatchets, and her bells, beads and copper; for they thought him as well of all occupations as themselves. . . ."

Smith then tells how Powhatan decided to send Smith back to Jamestown to ransom himself by obtaining "two great gunnes, and a gryndestone," twelve guides going along to bring back the ransom articles "for which he would give him the Country of *Capahowosick*, and forever esteeme him as his sonne *Nantaquoud*." When they returned to the fort, Smith relates, the two demiculverins and the millstone were too heavy for the Indians to carry, "but when they did see him discharge them, being loaded with stones, among the boughs of a great tree loaded with Isickles, the yce and branches came so tumbling downe, that the poore Salvages ran away halfe dead with feare." However, the Indians were sent back to Powhatan with other presents. Thus ends Smith's account of the episode.

Now all this may be exactly true. But there are some very odd and very suggestive points about it. First, it is odd that Smith's earlier account in the *True Relation* of 1608 does not mention the incident. But that could be due to the fact that the *True Relation* is a briefer account than the *Historie*, and John Fiske suggests that the text of the *True Relation* is incomplete even as Smith had written it—that the publisher omitted a good deal of material which for some reason he felt was best kept private. There is always a possibility that Smith actually told the Pocahontas story in 1608, and that the publisher struck it out. We cannot know, ever, unless from some forgotten pile of waste paper there should appear some day the actual manuscript as Smith submitted it to the printer. It is odd that Smith in his first account should say that he was convoyed home to Jamestown by four Indians, and that in his later account he should make it twelve. But that might possibly be no more than a mere slip. Most suggestive of all, of course, is the fact that the second account, with the rescue story, is sixteen years later than the first one, and appeared only after Pocahontas herself had been dead for seven years. The mouth of the only eyewitness who might have contradicted or confirmed the story was closed by death.

For Pocahontas had gone to England as Rolfe's wife in 1616, after having been Christianized and renamed Rebekah. She had been presented at Court by Lord and Lady de la Warr (Delaware). Lord Delaware was captain-general for Virginia, and he had an interest in promoting Virginia affairs which made Pocahontas and her attendant troop of ten or a dozen Indians a real publicity asset to him. Pocahontas was presented as the daughter of "the Indian King," raising an interesting question before the English King and Council of how Rolfe, a commoner, had dared to marry a princess. The King, Princess, and Emperor business was simply a little more of Smith's embroidery; Powhatan was in fact the quite able over-chief of several small Virginia tribes, but his scattered hundreds of followers were not much of an "empire." For a year before she died in 1617, Pocahontas was quite the pet of English society. She attended the Twelfth Night Christmas masque (by Ben Jonson) at Whitehall Palace, London, and her portrait in English costume made about that time by an unknown artist, hangs in the National Gallery in Washington.

Smith says he called on her during this London sojourn to pay his respects and talk of old times in Virginia. Evidently their meeting was a little strained, as Pocahontas was trying to live up to her new position and was probably embarrassed to meet one who had known her as a half-naked Indian child in the wilderness.

Pocahontas died while on the way to take ship to return to Virginia, leaving a son by Rolfe. Her descendants in this line (John Randolph of Roanoke was one and Mrs. Edith Bolling Galt, the second Mrs. Woodrow Wilson, was another) have always taken great pride in the association.

None of the other Virginia colonists in their letters home even mentioned the Pocahontas incident, though one would expect them all to have heard of it on Smith's return to Jamestown from his captivity. Contemporary writers do not mention it. Unfortunately the story stands entirely on Smith's own account in his *Generall Historie,* and "he alone is the herald to publish and proclaim" it. It is now generally agreed that this particular episode was an afterthought of Smith's in his later work, to capitalize on the popularity of Pocahontas and the general dramatic value of the tale. But it still has its defenders, and the stone relief sculpture which records the incident in the Capitol at Washington stands unmoved. This is one of the embellishments of history whose literal truth is perhaps not a matter of very great importance. Even if it could be shown, finally and forever, to be completely false, it would be unfortunate if it clouded in any way the very real accomplishments of Captain Smith. At worst it is no more than the very human impulse to add to an essentially true story "corroborative detail, intended to give artistic verisimilitude to an otherwise bald and unconvincing narrative." But Captain Smith was a greater man than Pooh-Bah, and one whose fantastically-adventurous career needed no embellishment.

Those who want to study farther this highly romantic American pioneer should, of course, first read his own *True Relation* and *Generall Historie*. There is a mildly humorous treatment of the subject by Charles Dudley Warner, *A Study of the Life and Writings of Captain John Smith* (1881). The first skeptic to doubt the story was Charles Deane in notes on Wingfield's *Discourse of Virginia* (1860), but on the other hand, John Fiske, in *Old Virginia and Her Neighbors*, accepts it, and so does Charles M. Andrews, whose *The Colonial Period of American History* (1934) is highly regarded. Dixon Wecter, in *The Hero In America* (N. Y., 1941) tells some of the interesting later ramifications of the story. One rather telling point against it is that *A True Discourse of the Present Estate of Virginia* by Raphe Hamor, the younger, though published in London in 1615, does not mention the incident at all. Hamor had been secretary to the colony, knew Pocahontas well, and referred to her as "Powhatan's delight and darling, his daughter Pocahuntas, whose fame hath even bin spred in England by the title of *"Nonparella of Virginia."* It would seem that he must have known of any such dramatic rescue at the time, yet he does not record it. Fuller's *Worthies* (1662) was reprinted in London in 1952, and is extremely entertaining. Moses Coit Tyler in his *History of American Literature* has a good discussion of Smith's tale as a part of early American fiction. Probably the wide acceptance of the Pocahontas story is due to the fact that William Stith accepted it for his *History of Virginia*, 1747, which was for many years regarded as the foundation-stone of Virginia history. Perhaps the most readable recent discussion of Smith and the Pocahontas story is *Captain John Smith—His Life and Legend*, by Bradford Smith, (N.Y.–Phila., 1953.)

It is interesting to note that a quite similar story was told of Juan Ortiz, a survivor of the Narvaez expedition picked up by De Soto. It is related in the *Narrative of the Gentlemen of Elvas*, published in Evora, Portugal, in 1557, with an English version later in Hakluyt's *Virginia Richly Valued*. . . . which first appeared in 1609 and was reprinted in 1611. This story was retold later in great detail by Garcilaso de la Vega (El Inca) in his description of Florida in 1723.

The human mind is naturally impelled to take delight in uniformity. . . . This axiom, as applied to the fables, is confirmed by the habit the vulgar have when making up fables of men famous for this or that, in these or those circumstances, of making the fable fit the character and occasion. These fables are ideal truths conforming to the merits of those of whom the vulgar tell them; and such falseness in fact as they now and then contain consists simply in failure to give their subjects their due. So that, if we consider the matter well, poetic truth is metaphysical truth, and physical truth which is not in conformity with it should be considered false. Thence springs this important consideration in poetic theory: the true war chief, for example, is the Godfrey that Torquato Tasso imagines; and all the chiefs who do not conform throughout to Godfrey are not true chiefs of war.

—GIAMBATTISTA VICO: *The New Science*

The Destruction of Historical Records

HISTORY IS, OF COURSE, NOT AN exact science. But that is not nearly as disconcerting as it used to be when we thought that science, at least, was exact. Now scientists themselves are talking in terms of probabilities and are, a good deal of the time, frankly guessing.

However, the goal of history is to be as nearly exact as possible, as nearly accurate as the data will permit, as nearly right as a well-tempered human mind can be. This means that the serious historian not only collects every scrap of information that he can find bearing on his subject, but that he cudgels his brain to assure himself that he has made every effort to understand and hence correctly interpret what he has assembled. Then comes the writing, of course, but here he is in the same boat with all other writers; that is, he is up against the stern task of trying to say what he means in terms which will assure that those who read will understand his meaning (and, if possible, not fall asleep meanwhile).

But what I am concerned with at this moment is the completeness of the record. A researcher reads and takes notes on every scrap of record written by his subject. He reads everything he can find about the period, the tangent events, the people concerned. At last he feels he is finished, ready to put it all down. Then comes the final, sickening thought. Has he really seen it all? Will there, the day after his work appears, be found a bundle of old letters, a cache in an unsuspected library, a forgotten book even, which he neglected to inspect, and which might throw an entirely different light on some of the things he is about to say?

This is not a mere type of occupational jitters. It is a fact. And at that sickening moment, he realizes that whatever his pains and toils, what he is about to write is incomplete; it does not represent the last word, and the last word can never be said at all. For, alas, the absolute and final truth about anything is known to the gods alone, and poor, stumbling, finite man can only make his uttermost effort toward it and hope for the best.

This is increasingly true. For the body of written record that clusters about a man of the latter twentieth century is so overwhelming that a man's life could be occupied in merely reading it, let alone evaluating it, putting it in its proper setting, and then interpreting it. Trucks back up to the Library of Congress every day, disgorging hundreds of thousands of letters, documents, papers, and correspondence that have clustered around political figures. The mere diary of a cabinet member alone may mount to six million words, like that of Harold Ickes, just a fraction of what one would have to read to obtain an elementary idea of his life and works. Recent Presidents, realizing the problem, have set up separate libraries merely to contain their official papers. To give some idea of the scope of the problem, it was announced in 1956 that the George C. Marshall Research Foundation of Lexington, Virginia, had received a gift of $150,000 merely to enable it to "*begin* work on the *compilation* of General Marshall's public and private papers." Not a week passes without presentation to the Library of Congress of the papers of some public person, each adding anywhere from five thousand to fifty thousand pieces of paper to the interminable record.

Now that is a problem of such staggering dimensions that I hear loud cries for the electronic brain. It may come to that. But in the meantime, let us look at the reverse of the coin. Let us consider the many cases where the record is incomplete, and will always be incomplete because papers and records known to have existed have disappeared, perhaps are known definitely to have been destroyed.

Losses of the latter kind are all the more poignant when we know rather definitely what has been lost. The great master-work of the Roman historian Livy (Titus Livius, 58 B.C.–A.D. 17) was his *History of Rome* (*Ab urbe condita*). This vast work is known to have been published originally in 142 books and to have been carried down all the way from the founding of Rome to the death of Drusus in A.D. 9. But of this vast mass of historical information, only thirty-five books have survived, with some additional fragments. There is, however, a summary of the contents, so we know exactly what has been lost. It seems likely that later historians have used material of Livy which appeared in the lost books, but we cannot be sure just what and how much. One of the perpetual dreams of historians is that the "lost books of Livy" may some day be found, and it is not impossible. After the discoveries of the scrolls in the caves about the Dead Sea which still lie under the examiners' magnifying-glasses, nothing can be thought impossible.

In fact, the "lost books of Livy" have already begun to build up legends about themselves. Holbrook Jackson, in his

Anatomy of Bibliomania, tells some typical stories of the lost books. One is that during a great fire in Constantinople, in which the Seraglio was burned, the Secretary of the French Embassy went to observe the scene. Articles of furniture, books, and all sorts of property were being thrown from windows to save them from the flames and the milling crowd of spectators was not averse to helping itself. The Secretary saw one man carrying a large volume and peering at it in a manner which indicated that he could not read. He stepped up and inspected the volume. He recognized the first and second decades of Livy, which are among the lost volumes, and he realized that this huge tome might even contain all the missing volumes. He had no money with him, but hastily and feverishly bargained with the man to follow him to his lodgings, keeping the book concealed under his cloak. The man agreed and they started off. But in the confusion they became separated, and the volume was never seen again. Were some of the lost books thus recovered for a moment and again lost? We do not know. There is another story that a man of letters recognized a parchment page from the lost Second Decade of Livy in the drum of a battledore. He rushed off to the maker, only to find that the man had in this way used up the last page of his Livy only a week before!

Other ancient histories which might have thrown light on the distant past have fared no better. Of Polybius we have only five of forty known books; of Diodorus Siculus only fifteen of forty, and only half of Dionysius Halicarnassensis. The opening book (as we know it) of Ammianus Marcellinus is the fourteenth; of Tacitus we have only four books of thirty. The Elder Pliny wrote twenty books of history, all lost. Varro and Atticus are known to have written hundreds of biographical sketches of prominent Romans, all lost. There is, of course, always a million-in-one chance that some of these lost works may yet be found in the moldering ruins of some abbey, some long-walled-up chamber, some forgotten and decaying box.

Man, the creator, is also man, the destroyer. On at least three occasions vast libraries of ancient manuscripts have been destroyed in Alexandria. Monastic libraries were plundered during the Reformation, and the pages of old vellum books and manuscripts used to stuff broken windows, light fires, or wrap packages. As late as 1870 there disappeared one of the best chances to learn details of the somewhat misty days of the first printing from movable types. When the Germans shelled Strasbourg, the library was destroyed, and in it were the records of certain lawsuits between Johann Gutenberg and his partners which might well have clarified some of what is now a rather hazy record of the invention of printing.

War is, in this field, as in so many others, the great destroyer. The repeated destruction of the great libraries at Corinth and Alexandria are examples from ancient history, but we need go back no farther than our own times to see war at work in obliterating the record. During World War II, some 59 British libraries were totally destroyed and many more than that were badly damaged; the British Museum alone lost a quarter of a million volumes. The same institution had a suburban warehouse stuffed with newspaper files from the eighteenth and nineteenth centuries, many of them unique. It was bombed out in 1940 and 30,000 bound volumes of newspapers were lost forever.

Fire, even without the aid of war, takes a continual toll. Our own Library of Congress, burned out the first time in 1814 when British soldiers took Washington, has been burned twice since that time, once in 1825 and again in 1851, the latter conflagration obliterating much of Thomas Jefferson's personal library, on which the national collection had been re-founded after the War of 1812. War, fire, and private neglect have wiped out an unknown proportion (probably a quite high one) of the historical record. William Blades, author of *The Enemies of Books* (London, 1880; 2nd. Ed.) says he believes that not a thousandth part of the books that have existed are available today. He then hastens to point out that this is not necessarily as bad as it sounds, for many of the lost books never were worth preserving, anyway. The difficulty is that the good go with the bad, and amid this staggering mass of "ghost" books, there must be many which represent a real loss. Again, we cannot know.

On the history of early America before the Spaniards came, there must always be gaps, and that needlessly, simply because men deliberately destroyed the record. The early American peoples in what is now Mexico, especially the Toltecs and the Mayas, kept elaborate historical records by means of paintings in strip form, rolled or folded. The earliest Spanish conquerors were induced by the priests who accompanied them to destroy all that could be found. Unable to read the records, the priests felt that they were idolatrous, and that it was a pious duty to destroy them. The Abbé D. Francesco Saverio Clavigero, in his *History of Mexico* thus laments this ignorant and wanton act of destruction:

"The Mexican Empire abounded with all those kinds of paintings; for their painters were innumerable, and there was hardly anything left unpainted. If those had been preserved, there would have been nothing wanting to the history of Mexico; but the first preachers of the gospel, suspicious that superstition was mixed with all their paintings, made a furious destruction of them. Of all those which were to be found in Texcuco, where the chief school of painting was, they collected such a mass, in the square of the market, it appeared like a little mountain; to this they set fire and buried in the ashes the memory of many most interesting and curious events. . . ."

Later investigators recovered what they could, but only scraps were to be had; injured and indignant Indians refused to yield up what they had saved, and we have only a few rolls of the thousands which made up that precious record, forever lost.

These Spaniards had the best of precedents. Religious groups have regularly destroyed the written works of opposed groups, as the triumphant Moors destroyed Spanish libraries, and the zealots of the Reformation in England destroyed those of the monasteries. They needed only to refer to their own Bible, Acts XIX: 19, to learn that when Paul came to Ephesus and swept its people with his revival meetings,

"Many of them also which used curious arts brought their books together, and burned them before all men: and they counted the price of them, and found it fifty thousand pieces of silver." (The equivalent of more than $100,000.)

Notice that these acts appear to have been voluntary under the stimulus of the new revelation, and that they are specified as being devoted to "curious arts." Nevertheless one suspects that the same test applied by the Mohammedans was applied here—that if the books agreed with the Koran they were superfluous; if they disagreed, they were wrong, hence in error, and hence better destroyed. In any event, today they would at least be considered "folklore" and hence eagerly desired.

But one need not go back so far to find losses and blanks in the historical record. Even the record on Lincoln, who was personally known to our own grandfathers, is not complete. Despite the four thousand books and pamphlets that have been written about Lincoln, we shall never know the whole truth. That is not only because of the veil that is always and inevitably drawn between one man and another, but because we know definitely that part of the written record on Lincoln has been destroyed. It is gone, and it can never be recovered.

The "authorized" life of Lincoln was that by Nicolay and Hay, his secretaries. Over this 4700-page book, Robert Lincoln, the only surviving son of the great President, exercised a supervision that amounted to censorship. It is known that he made changes and excisions in this biography as Nicolay and Hay wrote it, and that he retained in his own possession a mass of the source material they used in writing it. A quarter of a century later, when Senator Beveridge asked permission to inspect this material during the writing of his own (unfinished) biography, Robert Lincoln refused. He had an almost morbid preoccupation with his father's memory, and it was not the first time that he had attempted to color the historical portrait of his father. Robert Lincoln's whole life was overshadowed with the thought that he was unwanted as Robert Lincoln, and lived significantly only as Abraham Lincoln's son. Further, he seems to have been obsessed with the idea that if he had accompanied his father to Ford's Theatre on that fatal evening of April 14, 1865, he might have prevented his father's murder.

One night in 1923 a friend of Robert Lincoln visited him in his summer home in Manchester, Vermont. He found Lincoln surrounded by large boxes and piles of papers. The ashes of burned papers were apparent in the fireplace. He was destroying certain of the private papers and letters of his father. The guest was horrified and, after remonstrating, went immediately to call on Nicholas Murray Butler, President of Columbia University, who had just returned from Europe and arrived in the town. It was late, and Butler was unable to go to Lincoln's until the next morning. He did so, and found Lincoln sitting before a blazing fire, and beside him a box of "family papers" which he calmly announced he was going to burn. Butler remonstrated, arguing that any papers touching on Abraham Lincoln were not really personal property, but belonged to the people. At length Lincoln promised to give those that remained to the Library of Congress on the condition that no one should see them until 1947.

No one knows—no one will ever know—what he destroyed before he turned the remainder over to the Library. But it is thought they had to do with certain machinations against Lincoln within his cabinet. In any event, the papers given the Library were duly opened in 1947, without revealing anything really significant that had not been printed before.

That is not the only loss of Lincoln material. McClure's collection of Lincoln papers was destroyed by General Mc-Causland; others collected by Robert Levi Todd, an intimate of Lincoln, were destroyed by Todd Gentry, a descendant who had inherited them. Some were almost certainly lost in the Chicago fire. Southerners who hated Lincoln are believed to have destroyed many, and autograph-seekers, content to clip the signature from letters and throw the rest away, probably caused loss of many more. In short, deliberate destruction has created gaps in the Lincoln record that can never be filled.

🏵️

The records of other men have also been deliberately destroyed for various reasons. Tom Moore, the poet, destroyed the entire manuscript of Byron's memoirs because he felt that later publication of them would compromise the reputation of Byron. And Charles Godfrey Leland admits in his *Memoirs* that he destroyed a whole collection of material on Edgar Allen Poe which had been assembled by Dr. Rufus Wilmot Griswold. The latter had been unfriendly to Poe, and had collected material not only on Poe but on others, enough to form "the material for a book." Leland burned it all, feeling that publication would discredit not only the subjects, but Griswold himself.

Of course, the record is never complete on any historical character or event. Though we have thousands of the letters of Washington and Jefferson, for example, we do not have them all. Richard D. Altick, in his absorbing book, *The Scholar Adventurers* (N.Y., 1950) tells a story of what may have happened to some of their letters. It was during the opening months of the Civil War, Altick relates, shortly after the disaster of First Bull Run, that it became necessary to clear out space in the Capitol at Washington in order to billet troops defending the city. The space evacuated had been used to store government archives. In a long procession of sleighs, the records and papers were carried through the streets to be thrown into the Potomac. The winter wind tore loose some sheets, and passers-by idly picked them up. They were letters signed by Washington, Hancock, Jefferson. What letters and documents, and how many, filling what gaps in the historical record, were destroyed that day? Nobody will ever know.

Sometimes the destruction is deliberate, caused by a desire to protect reputations, or from an exaggerated sense of delicacy or privacy. It is widely believed among historians, for instance, that a great bulk of the papers of President Harding were burned by Mrs. Harding after the President's death. This took place in the midst of the scandals incident to the Teapot Dome oil leases, and at a time when the administration was heavily under fire. After the President's death, Mrs. Harding sent to Washington for all his correspondence, official and unofficial, and had it collected, packed, and shipped to the family home in Marion, Ohio. She then did the same with correspondence files of *The Star*, the newspaper of which Harding had formerly been editor, and even, according to Samuel Hopkins Adams (*Incredible Era*, Boston, 1931) wrote to people who had received letters from her husband, asking for their return. It is feared that much of this material no longer exists. But what is gone is gone, and it is usually difficult to show that it ever existed if it cannot be produced.

Edward Larocque Tinker was told, he avers in *The Bookman*, February, 1925, that even in a great New York Library letters and documents of Washington were deliberately destroyed because the lady who was in charge of them felt they were "smutty."

"I did not want them to become public and destroy the ideal of Washington that had flourished for so long," she told Tinker. "It was only a question of money. Could we afford to pay the price and then destroy our investment? We could, and did."

An accusation of such destruction is a grave charge.

Who gives to any man (or woman) the right thus to falsify the record? For, of course, to destroy part of the authentic record for the sake of whitewashing, leaving the whole record forever deficient, creates deceit just as surely as the forging of lying material and adding it to the authentic record. Either impedes equally the course toward the whole truth.

Aaron Burr has always been something of a puzzle to historians. He was a brilliant man, an outstanding military hero, he came within an ace of being President, and was Vice-President when his fatal duel with Hamilton ended his political career. His abortive expedition to the Southwest is still shrouded in mystery after 150 years of painstaking investigation. Was it treason? Was it sheer adventure? Did he aim to set up an empire of his own? Or did he intend only to extend United States' dominion? We do not yet know for certain. And the personality of the man himself remains almost equally inscrutable.

One of the reasons why we do not know Burr as well as we might is that Matthew L. Davis, his friend and editor of his *Memoirs* (N.Y., 1837) destroyed masses of Burr's papers. Let him tell the story (in the preface to the *Memoirs*):

"It is a matter of perfect notoriety that among the papers left in my possession by the late Colonel Burr, there was a mass of letters and copies of letters written or received by him, from time to time, during a long life, indicating no very strict morality in some of his female correspondents. These letters contained matter that would have wounded the feelings of families more extensively than could be imagined. Their publication would have had a most injurious tendency, and created heartburnings that nothing but time could have cured. . . . As soon as Colonel Burr's decease was known, with my own hands I committed to the fire all such correspondence, and not a vestige of it now remains. . . . I *alone* have possessed the private and important papers of Colonel Burr; and I pledge my honor that every one of them, so far as I know and believe, that could have injured the feelings of a female or those of her friends, is destroyed. . . ."

It is easy to understand how Davis felt at the time. But now, more than a hundred years later, Burr is dead, and the ladies who wrote to him—"malice domestic, foreign levy, nothing can touch them further." Would we today feel the shock at their letters which seized Matthew Davis five generations ago? Did Davis perhaps owe *us* something, as well as the ladies of whom he was so considerate? We cannot guess, because we do not know what was in the letters, and we shall never know.

Many of the examples of destruction of the record cited above are taken from Isaac D'Israeli's *Curiosities of Literature* (Boston, 1834 and other later editions), William Blades' *The Enemies of Books* (London, 1880), and Holbrook Jackson's *Anatomy of Bibliomania* (London, 1930, N. Y., 1932). Those who wish to go into the melancholy history of literature destroyed by the censorious, too often inspired by religious motives, may turn to *Burned Books*, by Charles Ripley Gillett, (N. Y., 1932, 2-Vol.). Nicholas Murray Butler's own eye-witness account of the burning of Lincoln papers is in Vol. 2, pp. 375 et. seq. of his recollections, *Across the Busy Years* (N. Y., 1940).

H. L. Mencken's Bathtub Hoax

ASK THE AVERAGE AMERICAN when the bathtub first appeared in the United States. If he knows the answer at all, it will probably be some compound of the following entirely erroneous information:

That the bathtub made its bow in America in 1842 in Cincinnati, proudly displayed by one Adam Thompson, who had been bedazzled by such a contraption during a European tour some ten years previously. That Thompson introduced his innovation at a stag party, during which the fascinated guests were actually allowed to try it out. That the medical profession rose in wrath against the device and denounced it as a menace to health. That there were various legal discriminations against it, ranging from sheer prohibition in Boston to special taxes in other places. That none the less, President Fillmore dared to install one in the White House in the fifties, and that he then and there took the first presidential bath. And so on.

Merely to give a thought to the idea that no American took a bath before 1842 is to dismiss the whole thing with an easy laugh. But a great many people read without thinking, and this set of nonsensical assertions has been accepted by millions of Americans. But that is not all. They have also been accepted by scores of writers who were in the business of knowing better, but who nevertheless industriously passed on the whole fable for a generation.

Fortunately this is one of the cases of historical distortion and error in which we know the whole story; we know exactly how and when this set of fables got started. They started in New York on December 28, 1917, when H. L. Mencken published in the *Evening Mail* a story headlined "A Neglected Anniversary." And the manner of it was this:

In the fall of 1917, Mencken's journalistic efforts had fallen something under a cloud, as a result of his eager espousal of the German cause before and during World War I. His own beloved *Sunpapers* in Baltimore had ceased (by public request) to print Mencken's stuff. An old friend, John Cullen, had become managing editor of the *New York Evening Mail*, (a paper now defunct) and he invited Mencken to write three articles a week for the *Mail*. But even he had to warn Mencken to "lay off" the war and to confine himself to amusement. Mencken, always versatile, flailed lustily about in all directions, demanding the secession of New York City from the Union, attacking poetry as a vice, and in general shooting off verbal fireworks in an effort to inject a little lighthearted fun into rather grim war days. Amid these pinwheels and Roman candles, there appeared the "Neglected Anniversary" in which the bathtub story was retailed in a solemn and scientific-sounding manner.

Mencken had supposed he had made the article so transparent that it would get a few chuckles and nothing more. He soon forgot the whole thing, and he supposed that everybody else had. At first to his amusement, then to his consternation, and at last to his horror, Mencken began to see his bathtub story reprinted, or its "facts" liberally used in the concoction of other articles. When an encyclopedia printed an article largely based on his "facts," Mencken exploded.

It was in 1926, more than eight years after the original article had appeared, that Mencken indulged in certain "melancholy reflections." He told how rewrites of his original article kept cropping up in newspapers and magazines, even learned journals, and at last in standard works of reference. Mencken beat his breast, cried *peccavi*, foreswore the whole performance, and hoped he had killed his brain-child.

But not at all. Articles based on the hoax continued to appear, and they continue to appear to this day.

Mencken, observing all this, became more and more firmly fixed in his philosophy that the American people can be made to believe almost anything—a conviction that distilled itself into two immortal sentences in the preface to his *American Credo:* "Truth shifts and changes like a cataract of diamonds; its aspect is never precisely the same at two successive instants. But error flows down the channel of history like some great stream of lava or infinitely legarthic glacier."

Curtis D. MacDougall in his *Hoaxes* (N.Y., 1940) has traced the repercussions of the Mencken hoax down to 1938 in considerable detail. An account also appears in *The Irreverent Mr. Mencken* by Edgar Kemler and, of course, Nathan and Mencken's *The American Credo* is a veritable garden of this sort of flowering of belief in the most unsubstantial of soils.

The Discovery of America

EVERY SCHOOL CHILD KNOWS that America was discovered by Christopher Columbus in 1492. Just as he knows that the first man to fly the Atlantic was Charles Lindbergh, in 1927.

Of course, Charles Lindbergh was not the first man to fly the Atlantic. His achievement, magnificent as it was, must be qualified to accord with the facts. The rapid development of flight during World War I produced planes capable of crossing the Atlantic. It was inevitable that someone among the first to try thereafter would succeed. On May 16, 1919, three U. S. Naval planes left Trepassy, Newfoundland. One of them, the NC-4, reached the Azores on May 17, Lisbon on May 27, and Plymouth, England, on May 31. That was the first Atlantic crossing by aircraft. But it was not a direct crossing. On June 14-15, John Alcock and A. W. Brown flew in one hop in a converted British bomber from Newfoundland to a landing in Ireland, the first non-stop crossing. A British dirigible, the R-34, crossed from Scotland to Mineola Field, New York, July 2-6, and then made the return journey, July 10-13. It was actually eight years later that Lindbergh made his famous flight. He took off from Roosevelt Field, Long Island, in the early morning of May

20, 1927, all alone in a small, single-engined Ryan mono-plane, *The Spirit of St. Louis*. Thirty-three and a half hours later he landed at *Le Bourget* airdrome in Paris. What made the Lindbergh flight immortal was the fact that one young man did it all alone, winning the $25,000 Orteig Prize for the first non-stop flight between New York and Paris. There was enough glory for any man in this fine achievement without gilding it with any inaccurate "firsts."

It is a little like that when one considers the discovery of America. Columbus discovered it, all right, in 1492. But was he the first man from another continent to set foot on the American continents? This raises a variety of questions with which historians are still struggling. It is a wilderness of conjecture growing out of myth, of reconciling known fact with misty assertions from antiquity.

There is, first, the thesis that America was discovered by certain Buddist monks or missionaries from China about the sixth century A.D. That would be almost a thousand years before Columbus. The story is that these monks sailed eastward from China by way of Alaska to a land they called Fusang, from a plant they found growing there and de-scribed, and which suggests the Mexican cactus or maguey. This thesis was first advanced by a French Sinologist named Deguignes in 1761. He said he had found in ancient Chinese historical manuscripts, the Year-Books or Annals of the Chinese Empire, a report of such a Buddist monk, named Hoei-shin, in which he told of his return from a long journey to the east to a land he called Fusang. Deguignes believed it to have been Mexico. In 1841 Carl Friedrich Neumann, Pro-fessor of Oriental Languages and History at Munich, pub-lished the text of Hoei-shin's record, with comments tending to support it. The whole thesis was then attacked by schol-ars like Julius Heinrich von Klaproth and Dr. E. Bret-schneider. The general verdict of historians today is that all these very early claims of discovery are not beyond the bounds of possibility, but that they have no solid evidence behind them.

Such, for instance, is the dim rumor that Irish castaways were storm-borne to the coasts of the Carolinas, perhaps during the sixth or seventh centuries. It is true that Irish monks reached and settled in Iceland, where they were found established when the Norsemen arrived there in A.D. 874. There is no reason why some ship of theirs might not have been storm-borne to North America. Japanese junks are said to have been driven ashore in Oregon or California. There is even a story that a Frenchman, Jean Cousin of Dieppe, was blown astray from a voyage along West Africa and thus crossed the Atlantic to Brazil in 1488. Henry Harrisse, one of the most thorough students of the era of discovery, dismisses the Cousin story with wry humor, saying that he feels sure the reader will pardon him if he simply elects not to discuss it at all (*nous pardonnera de les passer sous silence*). The Welsh have their Prince Madoc, supposed to have voyaged in A.D. 1170 to some land in the west where he established a temporary colony which passed completely from view. Partisans claim to find traces of Welsh language in Indian tongues, and references in Welsh annals. There are stories that a crew of Arabs, in the eleventh or twelfth century, sailed west from the Azores and found land that might have been the new world, and Italians, jealous perhaps that Spain had taken the glory of their native son, have advanced claims for the Zeno brothers, Nicolo and Antonio, of Venice. They left a vague report of having been wrecked in the North Atlantic, late in the fourteenth century, and having lived for some time in a place they called Frislandia, visiting another also, which they called Engroneland. They left behind a map which was printed in Venice in 1558, which was used by Ptolemy in some of his atlases and was probably used by Sir Martin Frobisher on one of his voyages. But efforts to identify Frislandia with America have been vain, and the whole tale is too indefinite to make much of a mark on history.

The Basques also have their claims, with a story that one of their sailors who had already been on the Newfoundland Banks aided Columbus. Even the Poles have their claim in one Skolno, and one may confidently await, in view of recent Russian developments, a claim from that quarter.

South America, too, has its claims. In a museum at Rio de Janeiro there are brass tablets found in northern Brazil which suggest Phoenician origin. And in 1827 there were found near Montevideo, Uruguay, a sword, helmet and shield of Greek design, together with certain Greek inscriptions. All of these have been used to suggest very early pre-Columbian explorations of America without providing any real historical proof.

All the whispers from the mists of pre-history await the production of any convincing evidence whatever. They are little stronger than the contention that Phoenician voyagers or their Carthaginian descendants reached America long before the Chinese monks, perhaps as early as 1000-600 B.C. From that we descend to the realm of pure myth, the peopling of all Central America from an idyllic island of Atlantis, now long sunk beneath the Atlantic itself. There is a whole literature built upon this myth, largely outside the realm of serious history, but fascinating reading none the less.

The discovery of America by Norsemen, however, is another matter. Here we can stand, at least from time to time, on fairly solid historical ground. For here the stories of westward sailing by Vikings meshes in closely with the known historical events in Norway and Iceland at the time. Political and military developments were such as to produce a known exodus from Norway of Viking tribes who had been beaten in war but refused to live in subjection to the victor.

The colonization and successful settlement of Iceland by these sturdy refugees is well established by the records, as well as their settlement in England and as far away as the Mediterranean. From Iceland, they next discovered and colonized Greenland, where Eric the Red established himself in 983. And Greenland, to speak geographically and forget social organization for the moment, is really a part of America. A glance at the map shows how a daring, maritime people established in Greenland must inevitably reach the mainland of North America.

And in the year 1000, Leif, son of Eric the Red, did sail across the comparatively narrow water barrier remaining, and saw the coast of Labrador or Newfoundland. He then coasted southward to a place where wild grapes were found in profusion, and he called the place Vinland. Nobody knows just where it was, perhaps Nova Scotia, perhaps as far south as Massachusetts Bay. Others followed, and wintered in Vinland. Then they vanished.

It is generally conceded that the Vikings or Norsemen "discovered" America in the sense that they voyaged thither, landed and even wintered somewhere on the northeast coast. But it was not a "discovery" in the Columbian sense of settlement and continuous intercourse with the sourceland.

Notice that I have said that the Norse discoveries are "generally conceded." There are doubters even here, who point out that the written record depends entirely on the authenticity of the Norse "sagas," and that while Iceland and Greenland are studded with unquestioned physical relics of Norse occupation, there has never been a single physical trace found in continental North America that is beyond question Norse—not a burial, not a structure, not an inscription.

When Ole Bull, the Norwegian violinist, started a movement to set up a monument to Leif Ericson in Massachusetts, it was long resisted, though the monument stands today. A Committee of the Massachusetts Historical Society protested that there was no reliable evidence to show that any part of New England had been touched by the Vikings. It added that "there is the same sort of reason for believing in the existence of Leif Ericson that there is for believing in the existence of Agamemnon—they are both traditions accepted by later writers; but there is no more reason for regarding as true the details related about his discoveries than there is for accepting as historic truth the narratives contained in the Homeric poems. It is antecedently probable that the Northmen discovered America in the early part of the eleventh century; and this discovery is confirmed by the same sort of historical tradition, not strong enough to be called evidence, upon which our belief in many of the accepted facts of history rests."

This being so, it is easy to understand with what eagerness those who believed implicitly in the Norse discovery version awaited some physical evidence that would confirm the tales of the sagas.

When a buried skeleton decked with unusual jewelry and weapons was found near Fall River, Massachusetts, in 1836, the Poet Longfellow remembered the legendary stone tower at Newport, Rhode Island, and wrote "The Skeleton in Armor." The skeleton was a "Viking bold," and as to the tower,

"There for my lady's bower
Built I the lofty tower
Which, to this very hour
Stands looking seaward."

Alas for romance, the skeleton proved pretty conclusively
to be Indian. Mysterious inscriptions had been found even
earlier on Dighton Rock, beside the Taunton River in Berke-
ley, Massachusetts. These scrawlings are an odd assortment
of pictographs, which look almost surely Indian, and rude,
letter-like characters which look like runes, as the characters
of the ancient Norse alphabet are called. Some of these
characters have been variously attributed to Phoenicians,
Norsemen, and others, including the lost Portuguese explorer, Miguel Cortereal, who is thought by some to have
carved the underlying inscription in 1511, the pictographs
and others having been added later.

As for the tower at Newport, it is still a matter of dispute.
It was known to many generations of Newporters as "Governor Benedict Arnold's Windmill." This Arnold is not to be
confused with the Benedict Arnold of the Revolution. This
one became governor in 1657, and left documents referring
to "my stone-built windmill." No early records refer to the
actual building, but neither is there any record of surprise at
finding such a structure already standing when the settlers
arrived. It has been shown that the stone tower bears a
remarkable resemblance to a stone mill in Warwickshire near
the original home of the Arnolds, but it has been shown in a
set of elaborate comparisons that the tower also resembles
certain Norse towers in Europe. Despite elaborate excavation
and investigation in recent years, careful study has shown
no very convincing proof of the origin of the tower.

Oddly enough, it is to a find two thousand miles inland
and several hundred years later than Leif Ericson that students turn most eagerly for evidence of Norse exploration. It

was in 1898 that Olof Ohman, his son, Edward, and a neighbor, Nils Olof Flaaten, were grubbing stumps on Ohman's farm near Kensington, Minnesota. Six inches below the surface, in the grip of the roots of an aspen tree more than fifty years old, they found a stone. It was about 36 x 15 x 5½ inches in size, and weighed 230 pounds. Two sides of it were covered with strange inscriptions. Ohman could make nothing of them, and took the stone to Kensington to be exhibited in the window of a bank. It drew some local attention and was at length sent to archaeologists at the University of Minnesota and Northwestern for examination. They at once pronounced it fraudulent and returned the stone to Ohman. Disgusted, he set it as a stepping stone for his corn-crib, where it remained for eight years, fortunately inscribed side down.

In 1907, Hjalmar Rued Holand, another archaeologist, came to examine it, and pronounced it genuine. Ohman gave him the stone, and he exhibited it for some time, giving lectures on his interpretation of it. He presented his translation of the inscriptions in an article in *Harper's Weekly*, October 9, 1909. At this time Holand took the Ohmans and Flaaten to a notary, where they set down their first formal record of the discovery, eleven years after it was made.

If Holand and others have correctly read the Kensington Stone, it tells that in the fourteenth century, more than three hundred years after Leif Ericson, 30 Swedes and Norwegians from Vinland had camped nearby and that a party of them returning from fishing had found ten of their men "red with blood and dead." It goes on to say that a party of ten had also been left in charge of their ship by the sea, a fourteen days' journey. It is dated 1363.

It it pretty useless for you and me, having no knowledge of runes, to form an opinion as to whether the stone has been correctly read or not. We can only note that some Norwegian authorities say no. Holand and others say yes. But it is only fair to note that in the fifty years Holand has spent in study of the Kensington Stone, he has made considerable progress in advancing its claim to being genuine.

In the first place, persistent search has turned up some other finds—holes bored in lakeside rocks for mooring irons, fire-steels, and axe or halberd-heads, all of which appear to be Norse. The nearest sea-point to the Kensington district is the mouth of the Nelson River where it enters Hudson Bay, about a thousand miles north. The "fourteen days" journey is clearly impossible for men traveling on foot through a wilderness to central Minnesota either by way of Hudson's Bay, the Great Lakes, or the Mississippi. Holand explains this by showing that a "day's journey" in early Norse literature meant an average day's sailing in a boat, perhaps seventy-five miles, which makes it come out all right.

If the accounts of the finding of the Kensington Stone are correct, and the tree grew above it, it must have been lying in the earth at least by 1848, probably earlier. But since Douglas County was first settled in 1867, if the stone is to be taken as a hoax, it then means that among the earliest pioneers there was one capable of engraving Norse runes in the style of the fourteenth century, imaginative enough to have devised the rather graphic phraseology, interested enough to go to all the trouble, well-versed enough in the Norse sagas and early literature to make the inscription and date dovetail neatly with known events, and enough of a geologist to know that there was once a lake in what has been in modern times a marshy flat. It is a tall order for a hoaxer in a pioneer Minnesota County.

A letter, first printed in 1888, only ten years before the finding of the Kensington Stone, indicates that a royal expedition was sent from Norway in 1349 under command of Paul Knutson to search for lost colonists of the Western

Settlement of Greenland. It is presumed that, finding the West Greenland settlement deserted, this expedition pushed on westward to Hudson Bay. The time is such that it is about the first in which joint operations by Goths (Swedes) and Norsemen were possible and it is precisely this combination that is noted on the Kensington Stone. There is no further mention of Paul Knutson in the Norse records; no sign that lands west of Vinland had been reported. This suggests that the whole party (except perhaps those left with the ship) was killed by Indians, or stayed on and became amalgamated with Indian tribes. The only tangible clue is the discovery in 1930 near Lake Nipigon in Ontario of what appears to have been a Norse grave, with the rusted remains of characteristic weapons.

Which brings us to strange reports of the Mandan Indians of North Dakota, the adjoining state. The earliest explorer in that area, the Frenchman LaVerendrye, noted "white" characteristics among the Mandans, and curiously-inscribed stones. Lewis and Clark heard of a "big medicine stone" revered by the Mandans, and such a stone, carved with strange markings, lies submerged in the Missouri River, and has been seen twice during severe droughts. George Catlin, one of the real students of the Indian, lived with the Mandans in 1832, and wrote that they had clearly sprung from some origin different from that of the other North American tribes he had observed. But the Mandans, a small tribe, became extinct in 1841 through the ravages of a smallpox epidemic, closing the way to any further study of their origin. It is another of those elusive matters, like the "Welsh-speaking Indians," the pronounced Chinese look in some Mexican Indians, and the "white" savages that crop up here and there in the world, that intrigue the curious, but do not really enlighten.

Those who believe the Kensington Stone to be spurious

have their own case. They doubt the local circumstances surrounding the digging up of the stone. They cite a Svend Fogelblad, a Swedish preacher and teacher, who died three years before the stone was found. Fogelblad once stayed with Ohman, they say, and was a scholar from Upsala University who knew runic and had books about rune writing. It is thought unlikely that any Norse party could have penetrated so far inland, or that they would have cut so elaborate a memorial stone to comrades killed by Indians who still endangered them. But if they did, it is likely that they would have cut others, and no others have been found. And, of course, some runologists dispute the reading and the genuineness of the inscription.

There the stone stands—at the present writing in the display window of the Alexandria, Minn., Chamber of Commerce, with an exact replica in the National Museum at Washington, and a vastly-enlarged replica as a monument just east of Alexandria on Route 52. But this silent stone has refused, after sixty years, to give up its secret in any form that is beyond dispute.

The most readable account of the alleged Chinese discovery of America is by Charles G. Leland, in *Fusang* (London, 1875). W. L. Wagener's curious little book, *The First Discovery of America*, was published in New York in 1863. The high priest of the Atlantis cult is, of course, the prodigious Ignatius Donnelly, whose *Atlantis: The Antediluvian World* was published in New York in 1882. It went through fifty editions. Donnelly (1831-1901) was deep in politics all his life as an elective office-holder, was a leader in the Populist and other reform movements, yet found time to write not only *Atlantis*, but *Ragnarok*, and *The Great Cryptogram* on the Bacon-Shakespeare controversy, as well as several novels popular in their day. He is a study in himself. One of the best discussions of the Norse discoveries is still

John Fiske's *The Discovery of America* (2 vols.; Boston, 1892). And Justin Winsor's *Narrative and Critical History* (8 vols.; Boston, 1889) is in this case and all others within its scope, an anchor. The last word on the Kensington Stone from its partisans is *Explorations In America Before Columbus*, by Hjalmar R. Holand (N. Y., 1956) to whom the stone was given by its discoverer. This book also has an absorbing discussion of the Newport Tower. A good pamphlet by William Thalbitzer of Copenhagen, *Two Runic Stones, from Greenland and Minnesota* (1951), is available through the Smithsonian Institution (Publication 4021) at Washington. Thalbitzer originally thought the Kensington Stone a fake, but now, after Holand's fifty years of work on it, believes it may well be genuine, though not yet proved so. Which is about where the matter stands today. *Conquest by Man*, by Paul Herrmann (N.Y., 1954), is the most recent consolidated account of the earliest voyages to America, and is an excellent summary, well illustrated.

But I do not write exclusively, or even chiefly, for the private use of the guild. The uncertainties of our science must not, I think, be hidden from the curiosity of the world. They are our excuse for being. . . . The incomplete, if it is perpetually straining to realize itself, is quite as enticing as the most perfect success.

—MARC BLOCH: *The Historian's Craft*

The Connecticut Blue Laws

To BE SURE THAT WE AGREE ON what "Blue Laws" are, let us try this definition: a set of police-enforced regulations that go farther than one likes in the matter of controlling purely personal morals and conduct.

The most rigid laws of this sort are not resented in a community in which all are equally devoted to the Puritan principles that prompt the laws. Such people would never think of calling them "Blue Laws." It is only when such laws begin to be enforced against large numbers of people who do not believe in the principles behind them that the term "Blue Laws" arises. A whole generation of Americans was led to connect national Prohibition with blue laws, largely by cartoonists who popularized the figure of the grim, Puritan reformer, and writers who blamed the spirit of Puritanism for the "experiment, noble in purpose," which failed at last.

Of course, it is well known that many of the early American colonies, and not only those controlled by Puritan influence, had some very strict laws of this kind, enforced by what seem today extremely strict penalties. But the ones we

83

think of in this connection are those of New England, especially those of Connecticut, and particularly a code of such
laws promulgated in New Haven. These have been printed
and reprinted, scoffed at and ridiculed, been made the
subject of scathing jest and learned comment. And most of
this comment is based on a summary of the New Haven
laws which has been shown to be full of imaginative errors. In short, they are based on an account of these laws
made by the Rev. Samuel A. Peters in a book called *A
General History of Connecticut by a Gentleman of the Prov-
ince*, which was published in London in 1781. He described
the code of forty-five sections as "laws made by this independent dominion, and denominated Blue Laws by the
neighboring colonies." Peters said the laws were "never suffered to be printed" because they were made known to all
by vocal repetition, but the "Reverend" before his name
forbade anyone to doubt his version of the laws for a long
time.

Peters was bitter about the Blue Laws. ". . . . they betrayed such an extreme degree of wanton cruelty and op-
pression," he said, "that even the rigid fanatics of Boston
and the mad zealots of Hartford, put to the blush, christened
them the Blue Laws . . . they were properly termed Blue
Laws, i.e. bloody laws; for they were all sanctified with ex-
communication, confiscation, fines, banishments, whippings,
cutting off of the ears, burning the tongue, and death. . . ."
He went on to accuse the Rev. Thomas Hooker of infecting
Bibles with smallpox, which fatal disease was then spread by
this means among the Indians. This grim invention of the
Reverend Peters has also been retold by those who did not
trouble to substantiate it.

Peter's account was widely reproduced for many years,
especially by those who wanted to disparage the Puritan

tendency to try to make people good by law. To moderns the laws make fascinating reading:

No one shall cross a river but with an authorized ferryman.
No one shall run on the Sabbath Day, or walk in his garden or elsewhere, except reverently to and from meeting.
No one shall travel, cook victuals, make beds, sweep house, cut hair, or shave on the Sabbath Day.
No woman shall kiss her child on the Sabbath or fasting day.
When it appears that an accused has confederates and he refuses to discover them, he may be racked.
No one shall read Common Prayer, keep Christmas or Saints' days, make minced pies, dance, play cards, or play on any instrument of music, except the drum, trumpet, and jews' harp.
Married persons must live together or be imprisoned.

These are fair samples of the New Haven laws as expounded by Rev. Peters. With their incredible severities, they provided excellent material for those who wished to deride Puritanism.

Now it happens that the legal records of Connecticut are unusually complete, and it struck some people as odd that this particular code should not be found in written or printed form among records which were so admirably adequate in other respects. At length Walter F. Prince of New Haven made a most laborious and complete analysis, which he published in pamphlet form under the title *An Examination of Peters' "Blue Laws."* He found that about half of the regulations set forth by Peters actually did exist in New Haven. He found four or five more that had existed in other New England colonies, but not in Connecticut. He found nine that contained errors, and eight that were completely spurious. It became evident that what Rev. Peters had done was to sweep together what he could find of Blue Laws from several colonies and add some picturesque touches from his own imagination, setting them forth together as a New Haven code that became known as "The Connecticut Blue Laws."

Nobody feels badly toward Rev. Peters about this, or accuses him of worse than too careless appropriation from earlier "authority," for Prince showed that at least twenty-eight of Peters' "laws" were taken from *The History of New England*, by Daniel Neal (London, 1747). But that merely pushes back responsibility for the "laws" and does not authenticate them. It merely adds weight to the old saying that "History never repeats itself, but historians often copy from one another."

A bit of study of the career of Rev. Peters by Evarts A. and George L. Duykinck showed why he had been so eager to make Connecticut look bad in the public eye. He had been born in Hebron, Connecticut, in 1735, and was a strong Tory when the Revolution approached. He was twice visited in 1774 by the Sons of Liberty, who on one occasion invaded his house in a moblike demonstration during which they threatened to tar and feather Peters. He fled to Boston, and then to England, where he remained until 1805. On his return, he was less than cordial toward his former neighbors in Connecticut, and no wonder. The Duykincks recited all this, and concluded, as to the Peters *General History*:

"Looked at as history, we may say it is unreliable; but regarded as a squib, which the author almost had the opportunity of writing with quills plucked from his writhing body, and planted there by his overzealous brethren of Hebron, it is vastly enjoyable and may be forgiven . . . a sober critic would go mad over an attempt to correct its misstatements."

They cited some of Peters' wilder stories, like that of the invasion of the town of Windham by an army of frogs and the description of strange animals like the whappernocker and the cuba.

This is not to say that there were no Blue Laws in Connecticut or New England. There were, and in other colonies as well. But they were not quite as savage as Rev. Peters would have had us believe. It is like the general belief in the burning of witches in New England, from which we still derive an expression that is most useful today—"witch-burning." Actually, no person was ever burned as a witch in New England. We quite forget that belief in witches in 1692, the time of the "Witchcraft Delusion" in New England, was not confined to New England, nor even to Puritans, and that at this same period ten times as many witches were hanged or burned in England as ever paid the death penalty in New England. (Millions of people in all countries still believe in witchcraft.) In that one terrible year of 1692, nineteen persons were hanged at Salem for witchcraft, but none was ever burned, and the plain fact is that the terrors attending witchcraft prosecutions in New England were far less atrocious than those in the parent country at the same time, Puritans or no Puritans. Further, the witchcraft obsession in New England was short-lived, whereas witches were still executed in Britain as late as 1722, in a long crusade which had over the years taken literally thousands of lives. As to the general severity of Puritan laws, it may be noted that in 1640 in Connecticut only twelve crimes were punishable by death, whereas in the England of 1607 there were thirty-one. At the time when Connecticut was framing its laws, larceny of more than twelve pence was a capital offense in England.

The Prince pamphlet cited above is undated and somewhat difficult to find except as reproduced in the Report of the American Historical Association for 1898, but there is a very complete discussion of the Blue Laws in J. Hammond Trumbull's *The True Blue Laws of Connecticut and New Haven and the False Blue Laws Invented by Peters* (Hartford, 1876). There is an amusing discussion of these and other vagaries of Peters in the *Cyclopedia of American Literature* (Phila., 1881).

Even a reprint edition of the Peters book in 1877, edited by Samuel Jarvis McCormick, failed to eliminate its inventions, for in reviewing this reprint in the *Methodist Quarterly Review* for 1878 (Vol. LX, 4th Series) William L. Kingsley not only referred to Peters as "a man who was utterly incapable of telling the truth on any subject," but dismissed the two editions with a curt "both are worthless, except for the book collector."

All advancement in intelligence and insight depends upon our ability to call in question and reconsider what we have hitherto taken for granted.
—JAMES HARVEY ROBINSON: *The Human Comedy*

Misquotations

ESPECIALLY IN POLITICAL, BUT also in literary, religious, and all animated discussions, we all like to fall back on authority. Just why people are not satisfied to say "I think this," but must always add "Jefferson said that" or "Lincoln said the other" is not clear except that we all like to add the weight of authority to our own opinions, in which it is plain that we have little confidence.

Thus the words of great men have become a sort of quarry in which later and presumably lesser men dig to find materials suitable to their purposes.

When the writings of Thomas Jefferson, for instance, are being published in fifty-two volumes, it is strange if in so massive a quarry one could not find a stone to fit almost any opening. But such quarrying is laborious, sometimes futile, and some have found it easier to fabricate for themselves the stones they want, and then to set them in some building of their own as the veritable product of the original quarry of genius. So we condemn our great men not merely to stand on granite pedestals for pigeons to roost upon, but we add the insult of perverting their words to our own purposes.

Lincoln has been one of the worst sufferers. Some of the words he never spoke or wrote have become almost as famous as those that are undoubtedly his.

Let us look at an example.

Americans arguing for a protective tariff have for many decades used a quite standard argument, attributing it to Lincoln. They quote:

"I do not know much about the tariff, but I know this much, when we buy manufactured goods abroad, we get the goods and the manufacturer gets the money. When we buy manufactured goods at home, we get both the goods and the money. When an American paid $20.00 for steel rails to an English manufacturer, America had the steel and England the $20.00. But when he paid $20.00 for the steel to an American manufacturer, America had both the steel and the $20.00."

Many variations of this quotation have appeared. Sometimes it is made to apply to other commodities, sometimes the prices differ. But Alfred E. Smith used a variation on it in 1934, the Republican National Committee issued it in 1936. Yet the most careful search of all Lincoln's known speeches and writings reveals no such statement. Further, Lincoln was shot on the night of April 14, 1865, and numerous authorities have agreed that the first steel rail ever rolled in the United States was produced more than a month afterward. It is a plain and impudent imposition, yet it has been repeated over and over again, creeping even into textbooks, and perhaps no one will ever know who first contrived it.

It will probably never die, any more than the settled conviction of all good Americans that Washington warned his countrymen against "entangling alliances." This particular warning was, as a matter of fact, Jefferson's. It is in his first inaugural address, in which he said, ". . . . peace, commerce and honest friendship, with all nations—entangling alliances with none. . . ."

But to return to Lincoln. Nearly a century ago, in the time of the Greenback movement, there appeared a startling, prophetic quotation from Lincoln:

"I see in the near future a crisis approaching that unnerves me, and causes me to tremble for the safety of my country. As a result of war, corruptions have been enthroned and an era of corruption in high places will follow, and the money power of the country will endeavor to prolong its reign by working upon the prejudices of the people until all the wealth is aggregate in a few hands and the republic is destroyed."

This one has continued to crop up from time to time. Charles A. Lindbergh, Sr., for instance, closes his book, *Banking and Currency and the Money Trust,* with it, and it was used as late as the 1936 presidential campaign. Yet this and another letter to Col. E. D. Taylor, commending him for activities in favor of Greenback money, have been characterized by Paul M. Angle, the leading student of Lincoln documents today, as "two of the most notorious fakes." Angle is especially severe with Emanuel Hertz, who adduced the baleful prophesy quoted above as having been part of a letter to William F. Elkins, Nov. 21, 1864. Hertz' book, *Abraham Lincoln: A New Portrait* (N.Y., 1931, Vol. 2, p. 954) is denounced by Angle as crammed with spurious Lincoln material. Other Lincoln letters which Angle regards as "proved forgeries" are those of Feb. 22, 1842, to George E. Pickett; of Mar. 2, 1857, to Rev. James Lemen, and of Dec. 22, 1859, to John J. Crittenden.

Domestic politics is not the only field in which words have been put in the mouth of the great to serve an end. One would not expect Lincoln or his alleged views to be a factor in Italian politics. But the attempt was made.

On April 2, 1920, Mussolini's newspaper, the *Popolo d'Italia*, printed the text of what it represented to be a letter of Lincoln in an Italian translation by Guiseppe Mazzini. This letter was represented to have been sent by Lincoln to Macedonio Melloni, an Italian patriot, and is said to have so agitated Mazzini that when he read it he wept and insisted on immediately translating it into Italian.

The letter urged the union of all Italy and the consolidation into it of the major islands, like Corsica. That just happened to be the policy of Mussolini's rising Fascist movement, and the quotation just happened to appear shortly before an international conference of Allied leaders who were to debate the territorial future of Italy. There is no question that it was felt by Mussolini that a letter of Lincoln urging his own policies would have some weight with Allied statesmen.

No original letter, no photostat thereof, not even an English text was produced. On November 24, Professor Gaetano Salvemini declared the letter, supposed to have been written in 1853, to be a fraud. He pointed out that it used certain nomenclature regarding local Italian territories that was not adopted, or even suggested, until some ten years later.

In 1931, and even in 1942, the letter was revived by Fascist political writers. No original, no photostat, had yet been produced. By this time American historians had become interested. They soon pointed out that in addition to the objections raised by Professor Salvemini, no copy of such a letter or reference to it had ever been found in Lincoln collections. There was no sign of any acquaintance with or correspondence with anyone named Melloni, and that the whole letter showed a familiarity with Italian politics that was almost certainly beyond Lincoln's interest or knowledge in 1853. The thing was an obvious forgery concocted by those who wanted to coin words of Lincoln which would serve their political purpose.

The deliberate forgery of a president's words, while almost immediately denied and exposed, had sufficient effect on American political thinking that echoes are still heard, seventy-five years later. Some of the seed planted by the controversy over this spurious document may even today be flowering in the McCarren Act.

James A. Garfield was a candidate for the presidency in 1880 when, on October 20 of that year, an agitated inquiry came to him from a California editor. Word had spread widely that a letter existed in which he had declared himself in favor of "cheap Chinese labor." It fanned to sudden flame a controversy over immigration policy which had especially agitated the West. Garfield asked for a copy of the alleged letter, and when he had read it, he immediately denied that he had written such a letter. But James Gordon Bennet, editor of the New York *Herald*, who had read the letter when it first appeared in the New York *Truth*, was inclined to believe it, and so were many other people. Even Garfield began to wonder if perhaps some routine inquiry had been carelessly answered by a secretary in such a way as to commit him. He demanded a facsimile of the letter.

"It relieved my mind," he wrote. "It is not in the handwriting of any person I know, but is a manifestly bungling attempt to copy my hand and signature."

Being a man somewhat shy of the rough-and-tumble of politics, Garfield tried to make his denials through party chiefs, but he was at last forced to make a personal statement.

"I have denounced the Morey letter as a base forgery," he noted. "Its stupid and brutal sentiments I have never expressed or entertained."

The truth, as always, has some difficulty in catching up with the lie, and in this case throughout the campaign many continued to quote the Morey letter. Garfield was elected anyway, but after the election he said on the floor of Congress, "Great as our victory was, I believe the forged letter cost us all the Northern states which we lost." It almost certainly cost him California.

But though this gross forgery was very quickly repudiated, the hand-made quotation continued to pass, and the bitterness it aroused helped perhaps to set a pattern of thought on the question of immigration which has not entirely disappeared, even today.

❦

Charles S. Parnell, the great Irish Home Rule leader, was similarly subjected to the wiles of the forger.

On May 6, 1882, two British officials, Lord Frederick Cavendish and Undersecretary Burke, were set upon while walking in Dublin's Phoenix Park by a set of ruffians who stabbed them to death. The murders were political, engineered by Irish irreconcilables.

Seven years later, the London *Times* began a series of stories on "Parnellism and Crime," seeking to discredit Parnell's Home Rule movement by connecting it with the Phoenix Park murders. On April 18, 1887, it presented the facsimile of a letter as Parnell's. This letter excused and condoned the murders, and caused the expected revulsion against Parnell and his movement.

The moment Parnell was shown the *Times* he denied the

letter as "an audacious and unblushing fabrication." But the revulsion against him and his whole movement was enormous. Parnell was able at last to get a special investigating commission appointed more than a year later. It found the letter a forgery, and the *Times* withdrew it. The letter was found to have been written by a wretch named Richard Pigott, a hanger-on along the fringes of political journalism, who committed suicide in Madrid as the police were closing in on him.

More recent times have seen the employment of this same nefarious technique of putting words into mouths which might hope to sanctify the words. In the time of the great depression of the early thirties, there arose in Asheville, North Carolina, an organization called the Silver Shirts, headed by William Dudley Pelley. This was a quasi-Fascist group, and its general approach to public matters was closely parallel to that of Adolf Hitler in Germany at the same time. On February 3, 1934, the magazine of the movement, *Liberation*, published an article attributing to Benjamin Franklin a violently anti-Jewish statement, said to be a reproduction of a speech he made to the Constitutional Convention at Philadelphia during its sessions in the summer of 1789. It purported to warn the country against Jewish immigration on the familiar ground that such immigrants lowered standards of living and morals, and never became assimilated, but maintained an alien culture. The Franklin speech was supposed to have been discovered in a diary of Charles Pinckney of South Carolina which he kept at the convention, and which had been discovered in the Franklin Institute in Philadelphia.

To begin with, it is well known that Franklin was on un-usually friendly terms with Jews, having once helped to build a synagogue in Philadelphia. And it was soon found out that the Franklin Institute had no such Pinckney diary.

What took a little longer to determine is that Franklin expressed somewhat similar sentiments in a letter written in 1753. But he expressed them concerning the Germans, not the Jews. It took unusual gall for a quasi-Nazi organization to take a quotation unfavorable to the Germans they admired and turn it against the Jews they hated.

A full account of the Melloni forgery appears in *The Abraham Lincoln Quarterly*, Vol. II, for December, 1943, in an article "Fascist Propaganda and a Lincoln Forgery," by Raymond G. Rocca. Any good history discusses the Morey Letter, but one of the more complete accounts is in T. S. Smith's *Life and Letters of Garfield* (Yale, 1925). Paul M. Angle in *A Shelf of Lincoln Books* (Rutgers, 1946) says that Ralph Hertz, who produced the Elkins letter in his *A New Portrait*, "was duped by more for-geries and fabrications than appear in all other compilations of Lincoln's writing put together." Several other doubtful Lincoln quotations are discussed by Paul M. Angle in the *Mississippi Valley Historical Review*, December, 1950, in a review of Archer Shaw's *The Lincoln Encyclopedia*. A good account of the Parnell case is in Joan Haslip's *Parnell* (N.Y., 1937).

Albert Woldman, lawyer and Lincoln collector, has some in-teresting examples of manufactured Lincoln quotations in "Lin-coln Never Said That" (*Harper's Magazine*, May, 1950). He says the "money power" quotation first appeared in 1896 in *A Gold Conspiracy*, by Stephen Nicollette, thirty years after Lin-coln's death, and adds a manufactured table of ten precepts of personal finance which sound much more like Franklin than Lincoln, but which were only recently prominently displayed in a popular magazine.

Ghost Writers

ONE OF THE FASCINATING
games that must be played by all who work in history is
"Who's talking?"

One would naturally assume that an autobiography is a
true fountainhead of information about the person whose life
is being written. After all, the man is writing it himself. The
information is right "from the horse's mouth" and it should
be reliable.

But even here the voice is not always crystal-clear. In many
autobiographies there is a ghostly echo, and every effort must
be made to separate the one from the other. This is aside
from state papers by men in political life, in which case it is
well known and understood that men so busy as the President must have help in the composition of speeches and
documents. That has always been true, but it is well understood that once such a paper has been produced and released
over the signature or under the authority of the principal, it
officially represents what he wanted to say. Both Madison
and Hamilton helped Washington to write his famous Farewell Address, but it is generally believed that the thought
is largely Washington's. Lincoln had his Hay, Johnson his
Bancroft, F. D. Roosevelt his Sherwood; Judson Welliver and

97

Charles Michelson left their marks on many a state paper. But public papers bear the stamp of those who issue them, and may be accepted as representing their thought. "Autobiography" is something else again. Here personal lives and events are being recorded and discussed at a more informal level. Yet even a man writing his autobiography sometimes does it with one eye on history to come, and may not always be entirely accurate (though even if he is not, something may be gleaned from the fact). But the autobiography that is wholly or in part ghost-written must be inspected with extraordinary care. It may reflect with utter accuracy the person and the events and opinions with which it is concerned, or it may not.

Let us take an example. In 1922, there appeared Henry Ford's *My Life and Opinions,* actually written by Samuel Crowther, the well-known economist and magazine writer. No one will ever convince anyone who has interviewed or talked with Ford (as the present writer has done) that the Crowther collaboration gives a true picture of either Henry Ford or his opinions. In the first place, Ford would no more have been able to write the book, stylistically speaking, than he would have been able to translate the *Upanishads* from the original Sanskrit. Ford's mind was a fertile one and he had some interesting ideas about modern industry and society, but that they ever jelled into as extensive, as complicated, as organized a view of those matters as Crowther sets forth, is open to the gravest doubt. How much of the book, then, is Ford, how much is Crowther? If such a book is to be used historically, it must be scrutinized and analyzed practically line for line.

Even Charles A. Dana, a professional editor and writer of the highest ability, was prevailed upon by S. S. McClure to let Ida M. Tarbell write his *Recollections of the Civil War.* Miss Tarbell is a queen of the ghostly world, a highly reliable and conscientious writer, and it is probable that the ideas and recollections of the book are all those of the imperious Dana. Yet Allan Nevins is among those who feel that a good deal of the personality reflected by Dana's "capricious, witty, sardonic, disillusioned *Sun*" has been softened to the point where it inadequately reflects the man himself.

When Charlie Chaplin's autobiography appeared in 1916, as *Charlie Chaplin's Own Story*, it acknowledged the "invaluable editorial assistance" of Mrs. Rose Wilder Lane, who, by the way, also wrote *Henry Ford's Own Story* in 1917, before Crowther took over. Assistance so invaluable as this usually means that the assistant did the actual writing. According to *Film Index* in 1941, most of the copies of this work were destroyed at Chaplin's request. To what extent could one rely on it as a source-book on the life of the great comedian who even forty years later remains a somewhat inscrutable figure?

Autobiographies of Frank A. Vanderlip, Evelyn Walsh McLean, and Walter P. Chrysler have been written by Boyden Sparkes, who is only one of the more prominent of an army of collaborators ranging from amanuensis to ghost in all degrees. Of course, it is to be presumed that once the subject has approved the manuscript, the work represents his thought. There is no reason at all why busy persons with a dislike for the drudgery of composition should not turn to experienced literary people to do it for them. But even assuming no distortion of fact or opinion, there always remains for the historian a nagging question in regard to the spirit of the whole—to what extent and how accurately does it reflect the man? Even the most skillful ghost cannot write a whole manuscript without rubbing off something of himself on it. There is probably a net gain, for we certainly get valuable memoirs of many persons who do not have time or ability to write them themselves. They simply present an additional problem for the researcher.

Not even the self-written diary or autobiography can always be accepted at face value. An example is the diary kept by Gideon Welles, Secretary of the Navy under Lincoln and Johnson. Welles had an almost unparalleled opportunity to observe from the inside what went on in those perilous days, and historians eagerly awaited the diary when it at last appeared in print thirty-three years after Welles' death. The editor, John T. Morse, Jr., published it exactly as he found it, without revision. But revision there had been, none the less. Welles had revised it himself. Years after original entries had been set down, Welles added material to strengthen or re-enforce, sometimes even to change the original entries. Close study of the ink of the original manuscript showed that he had made at least two revisions. What appeared in print was all Welles, but to the historian there is a good deal of difference between Welles' reaction at the time of the event and what he came to think of it years later. Everyone likes it to be thought that he was "right all the time," and while second-guessing is a widely indulged sport not confined to the political arena, the historian puts a different value on first and second guesses.

One of the most elusive ghosts of history is known to students only as "A Public Man." In the *North American Review*, the most scholarly and responsible magazine of its time, there appeared during the year 1879 extracts from a diary, covering events from Dec. 28, 1860, to March 15, 1861. It described men and events at a critical time in language so animated that it was felt that the anonymous author must have worked on intimate terms among them. It was a Lincoln document of importance, for as a result of several calls on Lincoln at the White House, the diarist told anecdotes and repeated quotations from Lincoln not found elsewhere. Other leading men and events in Washington during the outbreak of the Civil War are described with great pungency. The diary was of the utmost importance as a source of history if it was authentic.

But was it? Who was "A Public Man"? Was the person who signed his work in this mysterious way such as to inspire trust in his revelations? Were they actually a diary kept on the spot, elaborations on such a diary, or perhaps even a complete fake?

The editor of the *North American Review*, Allen Thorndike Rice, refused to answer inquiries about the author. The secret died with him, and neither his records nor those of the magazine told anything further after his death. Yet the diary showed such familiarity with Washington and its personalities that historians were reluctant to give it up. Eighteen years had passed, of course, since it was supposed to have been written, and some of the principals were no longer available for personal inquiry. Further, more than a hundred of the persons referred to were masked by initials, and thus were subject to mistaken identification. So the solution had to be found within the text of the diary itself, and inquiry turned to its minute examination. After all, the diarist made many references to himself, his characteristics, his likes and dislikes, where he was and what he did on various dates, the people with whom he associated. It was possible to paint a rough portrait of him from these references. This was then compared with those of people who might possibly have written it—with John Van Buren, son of the President; with Horatio King, Postmaster-General under Buchanan; with Charles Edward Stuart, Senator from Michigan; with Amos Kendall; even with Henry Adams.

Most of the possibilities eliminated themselves on one point or another. Views of the diarist on certain public characters did not coincide with theirs, or they were not in Washington at the time the diaries were written, or the like disqualification. The game was played, on and off, for a generation. But no really satisfactory identification was made.

At last, in 1948, Frank Maloy Anderson wrote a book which was the result of many years of historical "detective work." It was called *The Mystery of "A Public Man"* (Minneapolis, 1948). Anderson's story is a fascinating one for anyone interested in how a historical "sleuth" works. He tabulated every characteristic of the author revealed in the diaries, every mention of contacts with known people, with their dates. It required a trip to the British Public Record Office to find out from the papers of Lord Lyons whether the diarist had, as he said, called on Lord Lyons on a certain date in Washington. Amos Kendall was eliminated when it was found that he was in New York on a certain date when the diarist wrote himself down as in Washington. And so on, through an absorbing chase which threw a sort of police dragnet around the pertinent records.

Anderson concluded that the author was Sam Ward, known in Washington as the "King of the Lobby," and a brother of Julia Ward Howe. But he also concluded that the diary was either entirely spurious, a sort of hoax by Ward, or at least a fanciful embellishment of notes kept at the time. On both counts he believed it to be unreliable as a source of historical information.

Anderson's book was greeted as the solution of a mystery that had puzzled historians for seventy years. But five years later, a doctoral candidate in history, Roy N. Lokken, applied to Anderson's book and conclusions some of Anderson's own techniques. And he came to the conclusion that neither Ward's authorship nor the spuriousness of the diary had been proved. For example, there is a passage in the diary in which

Lincoln jokingly asks the diarist whether he had ever matched his height against Stanton's. Lincoln and Stanton were both tall men and proud of it. Every commentator had always assumed that this meant that the diarist was a tall man. But Lokken suggested that perhaps this was one of Lincoln's little jokes, and that the diarist was really a short man, making the remark a mere pleasantry. And so on, taking issue with Anderson on scores of points.

Thus, since it is not universally accepted nor beyond a good, strong argument, the matter of "A Public Man" must still be regarded as not settled; there remains a possibility that this ghost may yet be materialized in some form making him recognizable beyond a doubt.

The case for Henry Adams as the "Public Man" is made by Evelyn Page in *The New England Quarterly* XXII, for June, 1949. Allen Johnson in his *The Historian and Historical Evidence* (N.Y., 1926) has a good discussion of it, together with some of the general difficulties in crediting witnesses and gathering evidence. Anderson's book is cited above, but Lokken's criticism of it must be sought in *The Mississippi Valley Historical Review* Vol. XL, No. 3, Dec. 1953. The text of the diary itself was printed by the Abraham Lincoln Bookshop of Chicago in 1945 and by the Rutgers University Press in 1946.

Charles Michelson, one of the most prolific of political ghost-writers, tells a good deal about the work in *The Ghost Talks* (N.Y., 1944) and there is a graphic description of exactly what goes on during preparation of a presidential speech in Samuel I. Rosenman's *Working with Roosevelt* (N.Y., 1952). Though concerned chiefly with the literary rather than the historical ghost, the chapter "Speaking of Ghosts," in Vincent Starrett's *Books Alive* (N.Y., 1940), will be found entertaining. The literature of ghost-writing is notably slender because a certain "passion for anonymity" is part of the good ghost's equipment.

History: The Government Line

IT WOULD BE IDLE TO PRETEND
that governments do not influence the writing, as well as the
making, of history. Of course they do.

Every government has always wished its purposes to
appear noble, its policies well-intentioned, its acts effective.
This is not always an imposition on their peoples. The people,
too, wish their ancestors and themselves to look well in the
world's eyes. There are, therefore, wide variations in accounts
of the same events as seen through the eyes of the historians
of different countries. Vilhjalmur Stefansson, the famous
Arctic explorer, in his book *Adventures in Error* (N. Y.,
1936), wryly noted variances in schoolbook accounts of the
War of 1812 as he read them in a small town in Northern
Vermont and then in a Canadian town across the border, only
three miles away. "You would hardly believe it was the same
war," he commented. Or try inquiring in England for histories of the War of 1812. There, even bookish Englishmen
have never heard of it.

There have been some very amusing instances among the
inscriptions of the early Assyrian and other Near Eastern
kingdoms, in which certain kings, wishing to aggrandize the

fame of their own reigns, simply had the stone-cutters chisel out the names of earlier kings in a graven record and substitute their own, thus achieving a whole glorious history for their regimes with a few strokes of the chisel.

In totalitarian countries literally no history is written in the sense in which free peoples understand it. History exists there, not as a discipline of free inquiry, but simply as a supplementary means of indoctrination of people by the state. Thus in Russia, the memory of Peter the Great was anathema to the early revolutionists of 1917, but when the war of 1941-45 required a national effort, the history of Peter was rewritten in highly laudatory terms. Similarly, Trotsky, one of the greatest leaders of the early days of the Revolution, came into disfavor and was exiled. His story in all Soviet histories and reference books was promptly rewritten to show what a really dangerous man he had been all the time.

The most glaring example of all came in 1956 with the undeification of Stalin. For twenty years this Russian leader had been as close to the deification accorded to themselves by the Caesars as it is possible to come in the twentieth century. Stalin died, and on March 5, 1953, he and his whole regime became history. The record was written, and the record stood untouched for three full years. Then there was an abrupt about-face. Stalin was suddenly denounced as a tyrannical murderer by those in power, and especially by Nikita Khruschev, who had been at Stalin's right hand during all the events he now denounced in ringing terms. This necessitated an immediate rewriting of history within Russia, a hasty revision of all school textbooks, histories, reference works, maps, and even works of art. For instance, the book *Joseph*

Stalin, a Short Biography was distributed widely by the Marx-Engels-Lenin Institute in Moscow (U. S. edition, 1941). This was completely official, and stated that "Stalin's life and career are inseparably bound up with the career of Lenin and the history of the heroic Bolshevik party." He was "the brilliant leader and teacher of the party," and was noted for "his wise and practical leadership, and intimate contact with the masses," all of which he accomplished "in conjunction with his immediate associates" (including Khruschev). Into his own *Short Biography*, Stalin was in a position to insert that he was "the worthy continuer of Lenin's work or, as it is said in our party, Stalin is the Lenin of today." No one in Russia, of course, questioned this modest self-appraisal. It was "history" in Russia for twenty years.

Whether any really new historical evidence will be uncovered to support the new "historical" view of Stalin remains to be seen. The man had had thirty years of unrestricted power, with an all-pervading secret police at his service. No one knows what records may have been destroyed during that time, what closets securely locked. Yet even so, the denunciation of Stalin at home bore quick fruit abroad. On April 23, 1956, *Life Magazine* presented through Alexander Orlov, a Russian refugee, evidence that Stalin had been a secret spy for the Okhrana, or Czarist secret police, even as late as 1913, at a time when he was one of the trusted leaders of the Revolution. In the same issue, Isaac Don Levine, earlier biographer of Stalin, produced evidence that had led him independently to the same conclusion, which he later supported by a book, *Stalin's Great Secret* (N.Y., 1956).

If these claims are later substantiated by irrefutable evidence, they will necessitate considerable rewriting of the history of the Russian Revolution.

The so-called "Testament" of Lenin is a good example. This was a series of letters and documents of V. I. Lenin said to have been written in 1922 and 1923 just before his death. There was a letter written Dec. 25, 1922, giving advice and instruction to Communist parties, and characterizing Stalin, Trotsky, Bukharin, Zinoviev, and others. A postscript on Jan. 4, 1923, read, "I propose to the Comrades to find a way to remove Stalin [as General Secretary of the Party] and appoint another man more loyal, more courteous and more considerate to comrades, less capricious, etc. . . ." There was a letter on Georgian administration, and again, on March 6, 1923, an announcement of Lenin's severance "of all personal and comradely relations with Stalin."

Whether or how much of all this is authentic is very difficult to establish. Naturally, during the Stalin regime, it was either suppressed entirely or denounced as a falsification. But in late June of 1956, the ruling party in Russia published a series of versions of Lenin's "Testament," showing that he distrusted Stalin toward the last (though of course he *did* permit him to be appointed to the powerful post of General Secretary of the Party). Thus a record long known to the "outside world" became at last known within Russia itself. When even so well-established a writer as Gorky could rewrite his account of Lenin's views of Trotsky after Stalin had gained power, it is not surprising that lesser figures should have done the same.

A revised volume of the *Great Soviet Encyclopedia* issued in late 1956, noting U.S. intervention in Korea in 1950, failed to include charges made in the 1953 edition that the U.S. ordered South Korea to attack North Korea, and then supported the campaign with germ warfare. Soviet history, intent on down-grading Stalin, may yet admit what other history has always asserted: that the North Koreans were prepared and launched in their attack on South Korea by Russia (i.e., from the new point of view, by Stalin) and that the United Nations had something to do with the resistance to that attack. Perhaps history, Russian-style, may yet record that the sole factor in the defeat of Japan was not the Russian army, which struck Japan first on August 8, 1945 (two days after Hiroshima), and fought six days, until the Japanese Emperor accepted the Allied peace terms on August 14. It may even come to admit that the Allies were of some help against Hitler, and even in Russia's defense of itself against the attack of its ally, Hitler.

It is quite clear that the history of any totalitarian country (at home, at least) is just what the ruling clique says it is at any given time, and that the documentary record is just what successive regimes have chosen to leave undestroyed. It is needless to point out that, in any terms which free men understand, this is not history at all.

*

The rewriting of history, based on newly-discovered facts and on the re-appraisals of second thought and new generations, is a constant process even in democratic countries. But that is a gradual process, based on the balanced study of an increasingly clear record, and has nothing at all to do with "history" in the totalitarian manner. Since World War II there have been continual—one might almost say systematic —efforts to break down the reputation and fame of Franklin D. Roosevelt. But this is a quite different matter. The way is left entirely open for any production of new facts, or any re-interpretation of the old facts, with full confidence that time will winnow out the true from the false. It is not at all the same process as a sudden overnight switch which monopolizes all media and all points of view and by interpretation completely smothers the record, ignores it, or even changes it, at will.

All governments, including our own, have from time to time tried to influence the historical record. The difference is that any totalitarian government can go far beyond influencing—it can absolutely direct history, make of it whatever it wishes, without fear of any contrary version appearing to compete with it. And the free-world faith that truth has within it a strength that will eventually conquer error applies only "in a fair field," when the truth has at least an equal chance to put forth its claims.

As I have suggested, all governments are tempted to slip a foot into the tent of history. An example of how a government attempted to produce documentation to fit the case is in a letter from Adolphe Thiers as Minister of the Interior of France to the prefect of the lower Rhine (April 21, 1834). Thiers was engaged in suppressing a workers' insurrection in Paris and Lyon, and he needed "evidence." So he wrote: "I advise you to take the greatest care to furnish your share of documents for the great forthcoming investigations. The correspondence of all anarchists, the intimate connections between events in Paris, Lyons, Strassburg and, in a word, the existence of a vast conspiracy embracing the whole of France —all this must be made entirely clear." (Quoted by Marc Bloch, *The Historian's Craft:* Manchester, 1954.) How are future historians to look upon evidence presented by a man who himself became a historian, at such an investigation, and under pressures such as these?

It is not often, however, that one gets as forthright a confession of this sort of manipulation as in the case of Chancellor Bismarck of Prussia. His admitted tampering with the text of a telegram and his public release of his "loaded" text were the immediate occasion for the Franco-Prussian War of 1870.

In the early months of that summer, France and Prussia had been trembling on the edge of war, with a virulent, press-inflamed element in each country demanding battle. There was no more substantial cause than a diplomatic intrigue over the candidacy of Prince Leopold Hohenzollern, a distant kinsman of King William of Prussia, for the vacant Spanish throne. This claim, secretly fomented by Bismarck, was inadmissable to the French, who feared the prospect of Hohenzollerns on both borders of their country. As tension grew, Prince Leopold withdrew from his candidacy, and all real reason for immediate war vanished. But the French pressed their luck. Through their ambassador, Count Vincent Benedetti, they demanded that King William promise never in future to back any such claim in Spain.

Benedetti buttonholed the King on the promenade at Ems and presented his demand. The King, while perfectly polite, felt that "forever" is a long time and refused to give any such eternal assurance. Evidently a little nettled by Benedetti's importunacy, he told the ambassador that future communication on the subject would have to be through diplomatic channels. A coded report of these proceedings was sent through the foreign office councillor, Heinrich Abeken, to Bismarck in Berlin, with instructions to use his judgment as to its publication.

Bismarck was sitting at dinner on the evening of July 13, 1870, with his guests, Generals Roon and Moltke. Bismarck was meditating his own resignation, feeling that the war he had been promoting was being snatched from him just at the moment when he was sure he could win it. Roon and Moltke were glum; their "dejection was so great that they turned away from food and drink," reports Bismarck.

Then the telegram from Ems arrived and was decoded.

Bismarck saw his opportunity. He quickly asked Roon and Moltke whether they could win a war if it came immediately. They eagerly affirmed it.

Then, reports Bismarck, "in the presence of my two guests, I reduced the telegram by striking out words, but without adding or altering. . . . The difference in the effect . . . was not the result of stronger words but of the form, which made this announcement appear decisive, while Abeken's version would only have been regarded as a fragment of a negotiation still pending, and to be continued at Berlin."

Confident that his altered dispatch would have "the effect of a red rag upon the Gallic bull," Bismarck sent his version of the Ems dispatch to all embassies and the newspapers. Moltke and Roon cheered up to the point where they were able to take food, reassured that they would get their war after all, for Germans would read the dispatch as an insult to King William, and the French would see it as an insult to their ambassador.

That is just how both sides read it, and they got their war. It would be an over-simplification to say that Bismarck brought on the Franco-Prussian War by tinkering with the text of a telegram, but it remains true that he did the tinkering, and did it with the deliberate intent of bringing on war. It certainly contributed mightily to that end—one of the better laboratory demonstratoins of how government-manufactured news can be used to attain the ends of government. And if Abeken's original version of the Ems Telegram had not become known, Bismarck's version would have been history.

One of the books which had a decisive and unquestioned effect on history is the proved forgery known as the *Eikon*

Basilike. The Greek title means "royal image," or "portrait of a king."

This was a very moving account of the trial and condemnation of Charles I, with a memoir, presented as having been written by the King himself shortly before his death. It appeared immediately afterward, some say on the very day of his execution. It presented to the public so sympathetic and appealing a view of a "martyred monarch" that a great wave of antipathy against the Cromwellians began to rise, and swelled to the point where it resulted in the Restoration of Charles II. The government of Cromwell tried in vain to administer an antidote in the form of a book by John Milton, the *Eikonoclastes* (image-breaker). Milton suspected that Charles I was not the author of the *Eikon Basilike*, but his rebuttal was grounded in the defense of Cromwell rather than on critical study.

After John Gauden had been made Bishop of Exeter in 1660 (the very year of the Restoration, which suggests that he was being rewarded for services), he made an unqualified claim to having been the author of the *Eikon.* This was disputed by Royalists, who devoted most of their refutation to personal abuse of Gauden, but did little to diminish his claim.

Internal evidence, based on close study of the text of the *Eikon* set off against the known writings of Gauden, has satisfied most critics that Gauden really wrote it. Whole columns of similar or identical phrases and similes have been compiled, which are convincing evidence that the same man wrote both. The *Eikon Basilike* is not exactly a forgery, but it presented Gauden's account of the king, accurate though it may have been, as the words of the king himself. Therein lay its tremendous appeal and its sweeping effect on the history of England.

Even certain official records must be understood to contain conventional reservations. The Congressional Record is in general highly accurate, yet members often revise their speeches before they go into print, and clerks regularly expunge language that is deemed overstrong or improper. What was actually said on the floor may not always coincide precisely with the official record.

꿩

One of the most absorbing incidents of recent times in which governments were involved with the historical record is that which developed in Britain in 1924 around the Zinoviev Letter.

This was presented to the British public as a letter from Grigori Zinoviev, head of the Comintern in Moscow, to the Communist Party in Britain, in which he urged a plan to undermine the loyalties of the British armed services. It first appeared in the *Daily Mail* on October 25, 1924, and it can scarcely be without significance that this was just four days before the general election in which a proposed treaty with Soviet Russia was an issue. The defeat of Ramsay MacDonald and his Labor Party, and the subsequent rejection of the proposed treaty may have strongly colored the history of the succeeding twenty years.

Here again, no one has ever seen the original letter. It was circulated to newspapers and government people in copies, some of which showed slight variances from one another. The Conservative government which came into power on November 4 refused Parliamentary inquiries for a public investigation of the letter.

But it cannot be said that the Zinoviev Letter was simply

an enterprise of the newspapers, for before they published it, a protest against the activities suggested by the letter had already been sent to the Soviet *Chargé d'Affaires* by the British Foreign Office; almost immediately afterward, copies of the text of the letter were in the hands of various London newspapers. The Soviet *Chargé* insisted that the letter was a forgery, and asked for an independent investigation. After his government had fallen, MacDonald said in a speech that he could not be sure whether the letter was a forgery or not, but that it was suspicious that Conservative newspapers and the Foreign Office appear to have received copies of the letter at the same time. The new Foreign Secretary, Sir Austen Chamberlain, declared that he believed the letter authentic, but continued to refuse a public inquiry. Just as it began to appear that in some indirect manner the copies of the letter had been "leaked" to the newspapers by someone inside the Foreign Office, there appeared a Conrad Donald im Thurn, a business man, who claimed that he received the copy of the letter from "a friend in close touch with Communist circles," and that he then furnished copies both to the Foreign Office and the newspapers.

Thus the affair dragged on, year after year, with no original document to which the ordinary tests of forgery might be applied, and with Socialists crying "forgery" and Conservatives sticking to "genuine." In 1943, Arthur Upham Pope, in a biography, *Maxim Litvinoff*, asserted that the document had been forged by a White Russian emigre named Druzhelovsky. But Pope again supported his claim with very little evidence.

To this day there does not seem to be any very convincing proof either way. Belief in the document usually stems from one's belief as to whether or not it accurately reflected Russian policy, rather than from historical investigation into the document itself, and the document itself actually has never been produced.

Silence may be eloquent—more eloquent sometimes than words. Governments have sometimes remained silent as to rumors which they could easily have discredited, and thus affected the beliefs of millions, all with its effect on history itself. In the first year of World War I, it was widely believed that Russian troops were passing through England on their way to re-enforce the Western Front in France. All sorts of stories of sealed trains, strange uniforms, inquiries in the Russian tongue, went the rounds. But the British government, which knew very well the rumors had not a jot of truth in them, was content for a long time to let the rumors circulate, for it was felt the effect on morale of imminent re-enforcement of the reeling front in France would be good.

Germany likewise was content for its own purposes to let circulate a rumor that helped in a small way, at least, to lead to World War I. Several days prior to the fatal declaration, an airplane flew over Nuremburg. Amid the population, already tense with the nearness of war, the rumor spread that it was a French military plane, and that it had dropped bombs on the city. What seems likely is that it was a French commercial plane, but it is quite certain that no bombs were dropped. The German government was in a position to know this and to scotch the rumor decisively. It did not. Here, too, it was useful that people should believe a falsity. Hence the silence on the part of the government which was quite as effective as a lie direct.

The process of the un-deification of Stalin was unraveling itself as this book was being written; its sources are largely in the newspapers and magazines of 1956. For instance, the best discussion of the "Testament" of Lenin is in the *New York Times*, April 3, 1956; the texts as newly released in Russia appeared in the New York papers of July 1, 1956. Bismarck's own story of the Ems Telegram is told in detail in *Bismarck, the Man and the Statesman*, written and dictated by himself, (London, 1898). The best account of the *Eikon Basilike* is in J. A. Farrer's *Literary Forgeries* (London and N.Y., 1907). The story of the first large-scale American attempt to influence news (and therefore history) is told by George Creel in *Rebel at Large* (N.Y., 1947). Creel was the organizer and head of the *Committee on Public Information* during World War I and his story is absorbing, especially as regards such matters as the Sisson Papers, which are generally regarded as a forgery, but which Creel still insists are genuine. Kent Cooper, former head of the Associated Press, discusses many examples of government manipulation of news in *The Right to Know* (N.Y., 1956). While his conclusions seem to this writer at times a little too sweeping and oversimplified, his discussions of specific cases are worth attention.

It is true that the scientific reasons for preferring one piece of evidence to another are sometimes very strong, but they are never strong enough to outweigh our passions, our prejudices, our interests. . . .

—ANATOLE FRANCE: Preface, *Penguin Island*

Unspoken Aphorisms

IF THERE IS ONE QUALITY WE prize highly in our great men, it is their ability to coin a phrase, to cap brisk action with a *mot juste*, to die with an aphorism dropping new-coined from their lips.

So history is full of happy phrases that aptly point a moral or illuminate an act. The difficulty is that so many of them were never uttered.

My own generation is the one that was young at the time of World War I. And you will never convince any of us that General Pershing did not draw himself up to his most impressive military figure before the tomb of Lafayette in 1917 and murmur, "Lafayette, we are here!"

Not even the General himself can quite convince us, though after all, he was there. And he wrote his own report on the matter in Vol. 1 of his *My Experiences in the World War*. Perhaps there is no better guide to the actual event, so let us follow the general's own account.

On the Fourth of July, 1917, it was thought desirable to show Paris actual American troops in the flesh. There weren't many available, and none had yet been in Paris, so a battalion of the Sixteenth Infantry was brought on from St.

Nazaire. These were regulars, but the cadres had had to be filled out until two-thirds of the unit were recruits, and Pershing was not exactly overwhelmed at their dress-parade appearance at Les Invalides that day beside crack French parade units. (He notes that whatever the Sixteenth lacked in "spit and polish" it soon made up at the front.) President Poincare presided, and Marshal Joffre and other great French soldiers were present. The ceremonies at the Invalides over, the troops were marched off to Picpus Cemetery to the grave of Lafayette. There Brand Whitlock, U. S. Ambassador to Belgium, and other orators spoke. Pershing, who never fancied himself as a speaker, had planned to shunt off his oratorical duties on Colonel C. E. Stanton, a member of his staff who had demonstrated ability along this line. But Pershing was so urgently requested to say something that he did make a few impromptu remarks. It was at Picpus that "utterance was given to an expression that could have been born only of inspiration," as Pershing put it, "one that will live long in history—'Lafayette, we are here!' "

But it was not Pershing who said it. "Many have attributed the striking utterance to me," he wrote, "and I have often wished that it could have been mine. But I have no recollection of saying anything so splendid. I am sure that those words were spoken by Colonel Stanton, and to him must go the credit for coining so happy and felicitous a phrase."

Pershing's recollection was correct, according to Stanton himself. A nephew of Edwin M. Stanton, Lincoln's Secretary of War, Colonel Stanton was Pershing's chief disbursing officer. Recalling the occasion, he said, "When I reached the final utterance of my address, I deliberately stood at soldierly attention, and saluting the tomb, said in loud tones, as though I were calling to the dead, 'Lafayette, we are here!' "

The phrase had a peculiar appropriateness in that Lafayette was buried in Picpus partly in American soil. When he left America after his triumphal farewell tour in 1825, he carried with him a large chest of soil from Bunker Hill, and one of his last requests was that he be buried in that soil.

❦

Still echoing down from 1904 comes another brave phrase, "Perdicaris alive or Raizuli dead!"

A generation assumed them to be the words of President Theodore Roosevelt, and it took to its heart the man who could utter so uncompromising a defiance. Students attributed the phrase to Secretary of State John Hay, but in 1940 still another author was introduced, as will follow.

Ion H. Perdicaris was an American citizen of wealth, living in a villa poetically called the Place of Nightingales, on the outskirts of Tangier in Morocco. One night while he was sitting in the garden sipping coffee with his stepson, a Mr. Varley, a British citizen, and their wives, a group of brigands burst into the garden and carried off Perdicaris and Varley. Both governments, faced with threats from the chieftain, Raizuli, that the kidnaped men would be killed unless money was paid, set about framing protests and obtaining their release.

One day Secretary Hay sat in his office in the State Department composing a message to the U. S. Consul in Tangier. At this point Oliver Gramling, author of *A. P.—The Story of News* (N.Y., 1940) introduces another participant. According to Gramling, Edwin M. Hood, Associated Press Washington correspondent, entered the office to talk with Hay, who was an old friend. Hay showed him the draft of his message to the Consul. Hood sniffed and told Hay he was slipping. He then took a pencil and scribbled on a piece of paper his own journalistic version of how to put the matter in a few words. It read, "Perdicaris alive or Raizuli dead." Hay sensed the impact in the compact phrase and incorporated it in his dispatch.

The G.O.P. Convention happened to be in session in Chicago at the time, and President Roosevelt, also struck by the blunt words, sent a copy to the Convention on June 22. There it was greeted with loud hurrahs, and monopolized the Convention's attention for a day. "Just like old Teddy!" said the delegates to one another.

Perdicaris was released on June 27, and Hay noted rather ruefully in his diary, "It is curious how a concise impropriety hits the public." Roosevelt never claimed the phrase as his own (he does not even mention the Raizuli incident in his autobiography), but people simply attributed it to him because they felt it sounded like their impressions of him. Yet Gramling's account is based directly on records which he found in the A.P. files, and which he checked and found to be indisputably correct. Now we know that the famous words were not Roosevelt's at all, not even Hay's, but those of a newsman hastily transcribing diplomatic jargon into headline-ese.

One of the ringing phrases that has gone echoing down through American history is "Millions for Defense, but not a Cent for Tribute!" It expressed in nine words the spirit of the whole people at the close of the eighteenth century. It was reproduced on metallic medals and tokens, on monuments and in writings for several generations. It is as nearly immortal as a national phrase can be. And nobody knows who said it.

The circumstances are worth recounting. Not fifteen years after American and French troops had stood together at Yorktown to end the American Revolution, France and America were on the verge of war. For in the meantime, Revolution had also swept France and had degenerated rapidly into the Napoleonic dictatorship which rolled by military force across Europe and threatened England. The Directory, temporarily at the head of the French government, tried to force the United States to support it against England, and the new government clung desperately to neutrality, though a large party was ardently pro-French. French privateers began to prey on American commerce, raising all the issues of a free sea that were to be a cause of war with Britain a few years later. By 1797, more than three hundred American vessels had been captured by the French, and above 55 million dollars' worth of American property had been seized or destroyed under orders of the French Directory. American seamen were imprisoned and beaten. Several envoys from the United States to the Directory were not even received, let alone heard. President Adams, unswervingly for peace in the face of great provocation and opposition even within his own party, decided to send yet another mission to the Directory, and named C. C. Pinckney, Elbridge Gerry, and John Marshall. They found a situation of intolerable arrogance and corruption. Small European nations, terrorized by Napoleon's military successes, were being forced to pay large bribes to Talleyrand, the foreign minister, and to the Directors before they could even get a hearing. What followed became known as "The XYZ Affair."

After official rebuffs, the Americans were approached one day by a Swiss named Hottenguer, claiming to represent

Talleyrand. Hottenguer intimated that the Directors were annoyed at America and that money would be needed to cool them down—a little matter of a quarter of a million dollars. Napoleon's successes were pointed out: the continent cowed, England awaiting invasion. France might even declare war on the United States, it was suggested, unless money was forthcoming to soothe the Directory.

It was then that the impetuous Pinckney, pressed for an answer, burst forth. "It is no," he shouted. "No! Not a sixpence!"

The reports of these negotiations, published in America with the names of the French agents concealed behind the letters "X, Y, and Z," roused America to great indignation, and preparations began for war. The pro-French faction lost much ground; the country rallied behind the Federalist administration. On his return, Marshall was given a banquet in Philadelphia on the evening of June 18, 1798, by members of Congress. Toasts were drunk with unbounded enthusiasm. One of them was "Millions for defense, but not a cent for tribute!" And to this day nobody knows who coined that defiant slogan.

When Ethan Allen pounded on a door and roused a sleeping and half-dressed British subaltern to demand the surrender of Fort Ticonderoga in the early morning of May 10, 1775, did he really make his demand "In the name of the Great Jehovah and the Continental Congress"? He said he did, as he wrote the story later on. But there is considerable doubt about it, and some of his biographers, who have gone over the ground carefully, insist that what he really said was much more like "Come out of there, you damned old rat!"

Allen French, in *The Taking of Ticonderoga*, and John Pell, in his *Ethan Allen*, are among those who cast considerable doubt on the famous and heroic words. But the plain fact is that, except for his own version set down four years after the event, we do not know exactly what words he flung in the face of the sleepy and surprised Lieutenant Feltham on that historic morning. What we do know is that it was a daring plan, skilfully executed, and that the artillery seized at the fort, laboriously transported over the mountains on skids, helped to force the British from Boston and to win the Revolutionary War. Is that not enough? Must Allen also have thought up a bit of eloquence while doing it?

It is largely to Victor Hugo's magnificent description of the Battle of Waterloo in *Les Misérables* that we owe the proud gesture of the French General Cambronne, "The Guard dies, but does not surrender!" Hugo reduced this defiance to a single, unprintable word. Unfortunately for the slogan, the remainder of the surrounded Guard in the last hour of Waterloo did not die, and did surrender, Cambronne with them.

Galileo, muttering, "And yet, it moves!" in the midst of his enforced penance before the Inquisition, is a heroic figure, but even the *Encyclopaedia Britannica* long ago gave up on the incident, calling it "entirely apocryphal."

Whether Louis XIV ever said, "I am the State," or Francis I allowed that "All is lost save honor," or that Henry IV considered that "Paris is worth a Mass"—all these are in a class with Caesar crossing the Rubicon with: "The die is cast." They are legends, folktales; they are the kind of remark one likes to think of his hero making. They may reflect more accurately than anything actually recorded the true mind of the alleged speaker. They may, in short, be true in some absolute and poetic sense. But they are not history.

In addition to General Pershing's account of the Lafayette affair in *My Experiences in the World War* (2-vols, N.Y., 1931.), there is a brief account in the rather heterogeneous collection of sidelights called *A Book about American History*, by George Stimpson, (N.Y., 1950). A significant account of the American reception of the Perdicaris message may be found in Vol. 1 of Joseph Bucklin Bishop's *Theodore Roosevelt and His Time* (N.Y., 1920). Henry F. Pringle, in his *Theodore Roosevelt* (N.Y., 1931) rather makes light of the whole Perdicaris affair. One of the best accounts of the "XYZ" affair and the coining of the "Millions for Defense" slogan is in Vol. 2 of Albert J. Beveridge's *Life of John Marshall*, (4-vols., Boston, 1916). Ethan Allen's own version of his rousing words at the capture of Ticonderoga is set down in *A Narrative of Colonel Ethan Allen's Captivity, Containing His Voyage and Travels, With the Most Remarkable Occurrences Respecting Him and Many other Continental Prisoners of Different Ranks and Characters. Interspersed With Some Political Observations. Written by Himself, and Now Published for the Information of the Curious in All Nations.* It is as quaint and refreshing as its title.

On the breast of that huge Mississippi of falsehood called history, a foambell more or less is of no consequence.
      —MATTHEW ARNOLD: *Literary Influence of Academies*

Napoleon's *Memorial of St. Helena* and Other Forgeries

THE ANCHOR OF HISTORY IS THE written document. To inscriptions, to letters and notes, to material written by the persons concerned, the historian turns for the last word from the "original sources."

Yet even here he may be led astray, for the pen itself has sometimes turned dishonest under the hand of the deliberate deceiver or the sportive hoaxer. And thus the historical researcher is burdened with still another burden—the task of winnowing out the spurious document from the genuine, even before he begins his real task of ordering and interpreting the true record.

With forgery as a nefarious art, we are not here concerned —that is, forgery for direct monetary or literary purposes. What we shall consider is the forger's effort to affect the historical record. That such efforts began very early is shown by the chapter on *The Donation of Constantine*. But we had to wait for the nineteenth century to see exposed the most impudent forger of all time, if not the most effective. Vrain-Denis Lucas was an obscure Parisian clerk, but between the years 1861 and 1870 he sold more than 27,000 documents to Michel Chasles, an eminent mathematician and a member of the French Academy. Every one of them was an arrant forgery. M. Lucas ran the gamut of history, producing letters which he alleged to have been written by Pascal, Rabelais, St. Luke, Julius Caesar, Cleopatra, Plato, Sappho, and Alexander the Great. He even produced a masterpiece from Judas Iscariot to Mary Magdalene. All of them, by the way, were written on paper and in contemporary French.

How did anyone take any of this nonsense seriously? It seems incredible. Yet M. Chasles paid more than $30,000 for the letters, and fought bitterly for their genuineness throughout a long controversy in which the French Academy became deeply involved. At one time the boulevards of Paris streamed with people cheering for France and denouncing all those who doubted Lucas' documents.

Here again, Lucas played on a very common weakness— the desire to believe what reflects credit on one's country and thus, by derivation, on oneself. His first letters claimed to have been by Blaise Pascal, tending to prove that the French Pascal, and not the English Newton, had discovered the laws of gravitation. After a year and a half of controversy, in 1869, the French Academy leaned heavily toward sanctioning many of the letters, especially a set by Louis XIV which were couched in a style of such dignity and nobility that the Academy felt they had the true odor of majesty.

Then at last the letters began to be exposed to careful examination. For instance, it was observed that at the time when Pascal was represented as writing a letter to Robert Boyle in which he explained that he, rather than Newton, had discovered the laws of gravitation, Newton would have been only ten years old. That was the sort of slip which let the cat out of the bag, and in no time at all, the whole vast production of Lucas' industrious pen was shown conclusively to be utterly false. Lucas was sent to prison, and the impudent knave who had long held at bay the whole French Academy vanished from the record. Fortunately none of his forgeries can be said to have affected history, as they were too promptly exposed and not well enough grounded in learning.

As much cannot be said for certain others—for instance, those promulgated by Emmanuel Las Cases, one of Napoleon's secretaries at St. Helena. He wrote in 1823 a *Memorial of St. Helena* in eight volumes, and profited greatly by its sale. Because of his peculiarly close relationship to Napoleon as a secretary, his work was unquestioningly accepted, and many historians drew heavily upon it. Not until 1901 was it seriously questioned. Then Lord Roseberry in his *Napoleon, the Last Phase*, showed conclusively that at least five letters of Napoleon quoted by Las Cases were false. And they were concerned with important points. One, for example, was presented as being from the Duc D'Enghien just before his execution, offering his services to Napoleon. This was said to have been withheld from Napoleon by Talleyrand until two days after D'Enghien's death, the presumption being that Napoleon would not have ordered the Duc's execution had he known of it. It was an attempt to shift the blame to Talleyrand for one of Napoleon's more egregious blunders. At least four other letters were shown to have been forged, thus undermining the reliability of Las Cases' whole work, "an arsenal of spurious documents." And Dr. Antommarchi, one of the physicians who attended Napoleon at St. Helena, was found by Lord Roseberry to be no more reliable. "There seems to have been something in the air at St.

Helena," he remarked ruefully, "that blighted exact truth.
. . . There is a strange mildew that rests on them all, as in
the books and boots in the island."

Did you ever hear of the great Indian battle of Flint Top
in which twelve thousand Indians were killed? Even experts
on the history of the Ohio headwaters had never heard of it
when in 1945 the Greene County (Pennsylvania) Historical
Association published the Horn Papers. W. F. Horn, a
Topeka, Kansas, carpenter, began writing to western Pennsylvania newspapers about 1932, seeking publication of
voluminous records bearing on the early history of that
region. By 1935, Horn returned to the places of his origin,
around Washington, Pa., and became a sort of oracle, lectur-
ing on local history and taking parties on tours of historic
sites. In 1945 his collection of papers was published in three
volumes. There were the diaries of Jacob Horn and his son,
Christopher, old court and genealogical records, all supported by hundreds of artifacts, including lead plates dug
up just where Horn's maps showed they would be. The whole
pre-Revolutionary history of the Ohio headwaters region
would require considerable rewriting if these papers were
genuine.

In the following year Julian P. Boyd of Princeton wrote an
article in the *American Historical Review* (LI, July, 1946)
seriously impugning the Horn papers. Other scholarly authorities thought some of the papers might be genuine, but
that they had been so edited as to destroy their value to
history. A committee headed by Solon J. Buck, Archivist of
the United States, was appointed to investigate more
thoroughly, and in 1947 its report appeared in the *William*

and Mary Quarterly (Third Series, Vol. IV, No. 4). It found many anachronisms in language, a striking similarity in style common to papers supposed to have been written by different persons, and good metallurgic reasons to believe that the lead plates and most of the artifacts were false. It concluded, in short, that the first two volumes of the Horn Papers were so filled with spurious material that it was almost hopeless to sift out anything genuine. Only a few documents were presented as originals, and the bulk of the material proved to be copies purported to have been made in 1891 by Horn from originals no longer existent. But even this "original" material the committee found probably had been produced no earlier than 1930. In short, the finding of the experts was that the Horn Papers were forgery on the greatest scale ever attempted in America.

The odd part of this is that every usual motive for forgery was absent. The Greene County Historical Society of Waynesburg, Pennsylvania, which arranged publication of the Horn Papers, had done so after infinite editorial labor and the slow raising of $20,000. Horn himself got nothing out of the project except local prominence. And the Greene County people still insist that, though there may be some errors, the bulk of the Horn Papers are genuine and historically valuable.

The only really good parallel to this in earlier times is that of Charles Julius Bertram, who published in 1747 a volume called *De Situ Britanniae*, a highly detailed account of Roman Britain, complete with maps which proved as false as the text. Historians are only now uprooting the thistles sowed by Bertram in the fields of early British history, and some of his non-existent Roman towns and establishments were noted on ordnance maps as late as the end of the nineteenth century.

If some of the commonly-held American ideas about China in the recent past have not been too accurate, part of the blame may lie on the fact that one of the most popular books on China in the early part of this century was a rank forgery. It was *The Memoirs of Li Hung Chang*, the great foreign minister of China in the days of the Dowager Empress and the Boxer Rebellion. Li was undoubtedly the Chinese statesman best known to the world. He died in 1901, and when in 1913 his *Memoirs* appeared, there was great interest in them. The book won the approval of John W. Foster, President Harrison's Secretary of State, and it became highly popular.

Not until ten years later was it shown to have been entirely the work of William Francis Mannix, a newspaperman with a long record of fakery and shady journalism, who had confected it while sitting in a Hawaiian prison (serving a sentence for forgery, no less). Mannix had a long record of fakery in American newspapers. He had hung about the fringes of respectable war correspondence during the Spanish-American War and had later become a sort of fly-blown "old China hand." When he was in the Oahu jail, Governor Frear himself sent him the typewriter on which he wrote Li's *Memoirs*, and friends brought him the reference books from which he extracted his data. In 1923 the publisher brought out a new edition of the *Memoirs* with an introduction in which the whole story of the hoax was told, but unfortunately the one you find on the library shelves today is nearly always the 1913 edition, with no hint of its spuriousness (except on the Library of Congress index card, which warns specifically of the fakery involved). This is not

forgery, of course, in the literal sense of imitating handwriting, but the essence of the deception is the same.

For some reason never made entirely clear, a Lieutenant
R. D. Clarke became possessed by a desire to show Sitting
Bull, the old Indian Chief, as a man of vast learning and
talents. Shortly after Custer's Last Stand, there was published a collection of letters and poems by Sitting Bull in
seven languages, including Greek and Latin (but not his
native Sioux). Sitting Bull, the last great Indian, was shot in
1890. He was a remarkable man, all right, but not that
remarkable. Clarke's documents were the purest moonshine
and they found a final resting-place in the Yale Library,
where they are exhibited from time to time by the Jared
Eliot Associates, an undergraduate book club. With it were
shown Vrain Lucas' letter of Charlemagne, and others which
hold a permanent, if not honored, place in the Yale collections.

The New York Public Library, too, has a large collection
of forged documents. It has become customary among certain dealers in books and autograph material that when they
come upon one of the many forgeries of Washington, Jefferson, Lincoln, Poe, they turn it over the the New York Public Library. Gradually a veritable museum of mendacity has
grown up. It specializes in the work of Robert Spring, a
Philadelphia bookseller who turned to forgery to augment
the profits of his legitimate business. Many a descendant of
customers of Spring who bought autographed material from
him shortly after the Civil War brings it into the market
today only to find that Grandpa had been duped. And

another letter finds its way into the New York Public Library's collection.

The Library's "favorite forger" is named Martin Connelly, known professionally as Joseph Cosey. He has forged many Lincoln items but has never been arrested for it, simply because he has never misrepresented the item when he sold it. He diffidently pushes the letter under a dealer's eye and asks, "Do you suppose this is worth anything?" The dealer, seeing a chance to get cheap an article which may be genuine and valuable, buys it. Later examination reveals the Cosey touch, and the chagrined dealer turns the letter or document over to the Library, where it joins a large file of Cosey's remarkably skillful work. But all this lies in the field of the autograph rather than the historical document, for most of such work has not affected the historical record, nor will it so long as it remains, properly classified, in the New York Public Library's collections.

It has been noted that when there seems a definite need for documents—a desire to substantiate that which is ardently believed—the documents usually appear. Such was the case of the Lincoln letters and material announced with pardonable pride by the *Atlantic Monthly* in December, 1928.

One phase of Lincoln's life that has always drawn the romantic-minded is the young love affair with Ann Rutledge, so appealing in its tenderness, its tragedy with Ann's premature death, and the dark shadow it may have cast over the remainder of Lincoln's life. But very little is known, in detail, about this relationship, and it became naturally and quickly a part of the mythology that surrounds the towering

Lincoln, the gaps in the record being eagerly filled by art. So a real thrill ran across the country when the *Atlantic* announced the finding by Miss Wilma Frances Minor of "letters, passionate and real," which Abraham wrote to Ann and Ann to Abraham. There were other Lincoln letters, and the diaries of Matilda Cameron and Sally Calhoun, books used and annotated by Lincoln, and a mass of autographic and other material. "No reader will be more incredulous than was the *Atlantic* when the collection was brought to our notice," wrote the editor. The paper was chemically tested and found to be all rag. Experts passed the handwriting as Lincoln's. Dr. William E. Barton and Ida Tarbell, Lincoln biographers, were consulted. Miss Minor showed a quite reasonable line of descent by which the letters had come to her from Matilda Cameron, "a cousin and confidante" of Ann Rutledge, and from Sally Calhoun. The whole thing seemed air-tight, and the editors of the *Atlantic*, having taken every reasonable precaution, proceeded with publication.

The January, 1929, issue led off with a fine facsimile of a Lincoln letter to Ann, and the story and accompanying documents were unrolled under titles "Lincoln the Lover" and "The Courtship." The February issue was to conclude the series with a third part, "The Tragedy."

But another tragedy was already in the making. Paul M. Angle, secretary of the Lincoln Centennial Association, had already attacked the documents in a pamphlet and freely given his criticisms of the series to the newspapers. Critical analysis had begun as soon as the December issue had appeared and had mounted steadily. By February the *Atlantic* itself was badly shaken, but stood on its own convictions. But there were criticisms that could not be explained away —a reference by Lincoln, the trained surveyor, to a "Section 40," whereas no township in the area had more than thirty-six; and a reference in 1834 to Kansas, whereas that area was not known as Kansas until some twenty years later. There were many other discrepancies, some of which the *Atlantic* tried to reconcile. But by April the magazine turned over its columns to Paul Angle for "A Criticism."

Angle, not without relish, since the *Atlantic* had questioned his motives in the matter, proceeded to demolish the physical evidence, the line of descent of the documents, and the very existence of the Misses Cameron and Calhoun. He denied that the handwriting, spelling, punctuation, and general point of view could be reconciled with those of the known Lincoln. He felt it impossible that Ann Rutledge could have referred to the beloved Mentor Graham, the schoolmaster, as "Newton" Graham. And he concluded bluntly that "by no possibility can the Minor collection be genuine."

At this point the *Atlantic* left the public to judge. In almost thirty years intervening, no challenge of Angle's demolition has been raised. Yet there is still an air of mystery about the matter. Miss Minor could not have been influenced by money motives, for her contract with the magazine provided that she should receive nothing unless her Lincoln papers were accepted as genuine. There was never even any reason to believe Miss Minor herself was not in complete good faith—it is quite possible that the papers were just as the magazine presented them before they came into her hands. There is still a final chapter in this matter that remains unwritten.

Not forgeries at all in the sense that they might influence history, because in such cases the originals are well known, are the facsimiles which have caused many a heartache. Certain historical documents have been artfully reproduced and distributed, often causing people of later generations to believe they have the originals. How many people (thousands, certainly) have believed that they treasured at home a copy of an "original newspaper" announcing Washington's death? Well, they may be right, but the odds are very heavily against it, especially if the paper is the *Ulster County Gazette* for January 4, 1800.

No original copy of this famous newspaper was known until 1931, and only two genuine copies are known today. But because of the great interest in it, many copies were struck off in facsimile. Students have identified more than one hundred separate reprints of this newspaper issue since 1825. So many inquiries were received about it that the New York Public Library was forced to issue a brochure about it (by Dr. R. W. G. Vail) telling of the reprints and how to identify them. If your family is treasuring such a copy of the *Ulster County Gazette*, it *may* be an original, but the chances are very, very greatly against it.

The famous wallpaper newspapers of the Confederacy have frequently been reproduced, especially the *Vicksburg Daily Citizen* of July 4, 1863. During the siege of the city, the paper supply had been exhausted, and the *Citizen* had been reduced to printing editions on the back of wallpaper. When Union troops entered the city, they found the July 4 edition all locked up in the forms, but not yet printed. Printers among the soldiers, laughing at the defiant tone of the paper, which asserted that the city would never be captured, inserted a jocose paragraph noting their presence, and ran off the paper. Thus many copies found today are quite genuine. But nevertheless at least forty-nine separate reproductions have been identified, and the chance that your *Vicksburg Citizen* is genuine is not too brilliant. The playbill at Ford's Theatre the night Lincoln was shot has often been similarly reproduced.

No harm is done to history by these reproductions, but they have been a plague to historians and antiquarians who are continually being asked to separate the wheat from the chaff.

Though primarily concerned with the literary rather than the historical field, the standard book on this subject is J. A. Farrer's *Literary Forgeries* (N. Y., 1907). There is much interesting material on forgery in Mary A. Benjamin's *Autographs* (N. Y., 1946), though her interest is chiefly in authentic signatures rather than in historical sources. The technical aspects of the detection of forgery are thoroughly detailed in Captain Arthur J. Quirke's *Forged, Anonymous, and Suspect Documents* (London, 1930).

Not only Lincoln but also Cotton Mather and George Washington himself were victims of the perfidious pen. The scandalous forged letters and papers used in an attempt to discredit Washington are discussed by John C. Fitzpatrick in Bulletin No. 1 of the Washington Society of Alexandria, in an article expanded from a previous similar article in *Scribner's*. The forged letter involving Cotton Mather in a scheme to capture 100 or more Quakers from a ship at sea, and sell them in Barbados for rum and sugar, had already been exposed by 1870, and again in 1908; and finally in Thomas J. Holmes' *Cotton Mather Bibliography*, Vol. III, Appendix A, 1940, which reproduces both the alleged letter and an account of it.

The Body of John Wilkes Booth

WHEN I WAS A BOY, AROUND
1910, one of the events of the long summer vacation was the
Summit County (Ohio) Fair. We went to the fair to absorb
not only quantities of taffy and lukewarm raspberry pop,
but education as well. Were not Eli, the Cigarette Fiend, and
the Tattooed Man educational as well as entertaining? They
were, but we got a lesson in history, too. In one tent there
was shown to the gaping youth of the community the
mummy of John Wilkes Booth, the man who murdered
Lincoln. And with it, at no extra cost, there was presented
the barker's story of how Booth was not shot and captured
by his pursuers, but escaped, lived a long life, and on dying
under the name of St. Helen, his body was embalmed, and
was before us in miraculously mummified form. Who could
doubt the tale? There lay the mummy!

The barker had his chance at me before the professional
historians. And though the historians have repeatedly assured me that Booth died as their books say he did, I have
never quite rooted out of a corner of my mind the sideshow
tent and the mummy. Probably hundreds of thousands of
Americans of my generation saw it, and certainly a great

137

many came away with some little tinge of doubt left in their minds. And truly, the circumstances of Lincoln's death and the pursuit of Booth were fraught with mystery, the circumstances strange enough to warrant their re-examination in books written as the result of long research in recent years. Even the slightest degree of mystery beclouding the death of a prominent person begets its inevitable cloud of rumors.

The tragic death of Lincoln has been carefully re-examined only recently. Let us see what lies behind the rumors about Booth. They had their origin, of course, in the days of helpless terror and almost primitive passion that swept the country with news of the murder of the beloved "Father Abraham." During the night of April 26-27, 1865, Union soldiers in pursuit of Booth carried from Richard Garrett's burning barn in Caroline County, Virginia, a man dying of a gunshot wound. He may have been shot by Boston Corbett, one of the soldiers, in disregard of instructions to capture him alive; he may have shot himself. He died at dawn, and the government announced that he was John Wilkes Booth. It then proceeded to dispose of the body in a manner that could scarcely have been improved upon if the purpose had been to arouse suspicion and generate rumor.

First, Colonel E. J. Conger, assistant to Col. Lafayette C. Baker, Chief of the Secret Service, searched the dying man's pockets and set off in haste for Washington with the news and the product of his search, including Booth's diary. As soon as Booth had died and a local doctor had been found to confirm the fact, the body was wrapped in a blanket, loaded into a farm wagon, and taken to the Potomac. There a steamer took the whole party aboard for Washington. As they reached Alexandria, a tug pulled alongside and the body, as well as the captive, David E. Herold, taken in the barn with the dead man, were put aboard the tug in the charge of the Secret Service. All were then transferred to the Ironclad *Montauk*, where the other arrested conspirators were already closely confined, loaded with hideous irons.

The body of the dead man lay on the *Montauk*'s deck through all the next day. No one in the capital but the heads of the Secret Service had thus far seen the body, and immediately the rumor spread through the city that there was something fishy about the matter. In the afternoon there came aboard a committee from Secretary Stanton to identify the body formally. It included Charles Dawson, room clerk at the hotel where Booth had been staying, and Dr. John Frederick May, who had once removed a tumor from Booth's neck. No record of the proceedings was made public—nothing but a bare announcement that the identification had been made.

Crowds of people stood along the shore, staring at the *Montauk*. Evidently there was fear that Southern sympathizers in Washington would try to obtain relics, locks of hair, clothing, from the body for some nameless "shrine" of the future. So Colonel Baker was ordered to make summary and secret disposition of the body. He indulged in a bit of dramatics which again swelled the chorus of "Mystery." At sunset, in full view of the crowd on shore, a coffin-like ammunition box and a heavy ball and chain were lowered into a rowboat. The tiny rowboat drifted downstream, and the crowd tried to follow it on shore. But the boat, a couple of miles below, was rowed into the swamp which then lay below Giesboro Point, a dismal and dangerous area which the people on shore could not approach. The rowboat vanished from sight.

What it did after eluding the watchers was to pull upstream to the old penitentiary, then used as an arsenal. There the body was buried under a warehouse floor in a locked room. But because Colonel Baker refused to give any information whatsoever, every rumor-monger had a field day, and every possible conjecture was made and spread abroad to an eager populace. Prominent among the rumors was one to the effect that the wrong man had been shot, but that in order to cover up the mistake and cash in on the $50,000 reward, this could not be admitted; hence, the body had been quickly placed beyond the possibility of any further check-up.

The rumors hatched by this mysterious proceeding in Washington in 1865 continued to flower among two generations of Americans.

Five years later, in February of 1869, the government yielded to requests of the Booth family for the body of their ill-starred kinsman. Members of the family identified the body, insofar as that was then still possible, pronounced themselves satisfied, and buried it without a headstone in the family plot in Baltimore.

But whispered talk had distilled itself into print before even a year was out. Reports began to be published of people who had seen Booth—in the South, on ships bound for South America. Certain newspapers flatly charged that Baker and his associates had swindled the public for the reward, and cited three instances in which Booth had been seen. The family identification in 1869 was also handled in a somewhat mysterious and semi-secret way, because of Edwin Booth's understandable sensitiveness. Instead of solving the mystery once and for all, it only added to the doubts. These grew and spread. They reached a point where any slim, pale man with long, dark hair and a slight limp was apt to be pointed out as Booth. Such a one was a Rev. J. G. Armstrong of Richmond, Virginia, many of whose parishioners there, and later in Atlanta, believed him to have been Booth. His death, with revelation of his complete life story, utterly disproved the tale. No fewer than twenty men were actively suspected at various times and places of being Booth. The theory was that Booth had fled into the woods at the approach of the Union cavalry, and that the man caught in the barn with Herold and shot was a mere tramp, unconnected with the Lincoln tragedy.

It was not until the late '70's that the most realistic claimant of all appeared. In Granbury, Texas, there was a saloon-keeper who, when he had liberally patronized his own bar, was apt to tell bystanders that he was Booth. He was known locally as John St. Helen, and he had a scar on the back of his neck, though there were those who were pretty sure it was the mark of a brawl in his own saloon. Finis L. Bates, a Memphis lawyer, who had heard the tale as a youth from St. Helen, never forgot it, and as a man he remembered it vividly when he heard of the suicide in Enid, Oklahoma, of one David E. George, who had made a similar claim. Bates went to Enid, found George's body on display before a popeyed multitude, and decided that George was St. Helen, and that both were Booth. He had the body preserved and exhibited, and in 1907 published a book which circulated widely for many years—*The Escape and Suicide of John Wilkes Booth, or The First True Account of Lincoln's Assassination, Containing a Complete Confession by Booth, Many Years after His Crime.* The embalmed or mummified body on exhibit was subjected to x-ray examination, and Bates claimed it showed the broken leg which Booth injured in vaulting from the fatal box at Ford's Theatre, as well as a ring in the stomach with initials variously read as "J" or "B." Bates does not seem to have been the sort of charlatan usually connected with this sort of exhibit, but to have been sincere and to have made considerable effort to substantiate his story by investigation. But, of course, no qualified authority ever gave the slightest credence to the mummified Booth.

In 1925, at least twenty-five different skulls were being shown with the claim that they were Booth's (just as at least two hundred proud owners display the pistol with which Booth fired the fatal shot). But it was not until 1937 that there appeared the strangest story of all. In that year Izola Forrester published a book, *This One Mad Act*, in which she asserted that she was Booth's granddaughter by a marriage of Booth before the Civil War, that Booth had been the tool of the Knights of the Golden Circle, who had really instigated the Lincoln murder and had contrived Booth's escape, and that Booth himself lived in seclusion until 1879. Her mother, Ogarita or "Rita" Booth, was the daughter of John Wilkes Booth. She was an actress, as was Izola, and was known as Booth's daughter, as clippings preserved by the family showed. Izola tells of an affecting incident of her mother's indignant despair at finding herself billed as "daughter of the assassin, John Wilkes Booth." Izola, the granddaughter, inspired by various family traditions and keepsakes, spent forty years investigating the story of the man she had learned to regard as her grandfather. She denied the St. Helen story as presented by Bates, but worked out a somewhat similar version of Booth's alleged escape from the Garrett barn just before the troopers arrived.

The story of Booth's escape, denied by every reputable historian, has had a strange persistence for more than ninety years. The historians demand evidence, and of the "escape" of Booth there is no direct evidence whatever. On the other hand, evidence of the identification of the body is all but conclusive. Yet it lacks the touch of finality, and the whole proceeding is still enveloped in the hysteria, the terror, the almost mad miasma which for a few weeks after the assassination benumbed the whole country. So much remains unexplained in this short sequence of events that they have been investigated and re-investigated, combed and sifted, again and again, without conclusively changing any of the central facts, and yet without removing even from the minds of some very competent scholars the distinct impression that there are yet untold stories lurking in the fog.

The story of Abraham Lincoln, as it is known to the average American, is part history, part saga, part myth. In all these aspects he is great, and in all he is a valid and living part of the soul of America. We have just discussed a single one of the myths that have clustered about him. Others are well told in *The Great American Myth*, by George S. Bryan (N. Y., 1940) and in Lloyd Lewis' remarkable series of studies, *Myths after Lincoln* (N.Y., 1929). The events surrounding his tragic death have been repeatedly studied and assayed, in Francis Wilson's *John Wilkes Booth: Fact and Fiction of Lincoln's Assassination* (Boston, 1929), and again in great detail in *Why Was Lincoln Murdered?* by Otto Eisenschiml (Boston, 1937), and *The Day Lincoln Was Shot* by James Alonzo Bishop (N. Y., 1955).

The complete title of Izola Forrester's fascinating though somewhat unconvincing book is *This One Mad Act, the Unknown Story of John Wilkes Booth and His Family by His Granddaughter* (Boston, 1937). It makes an interesting contrast to Philip Van Doren Stern's *The Man Who Killed Lincoln* (N. Y., 1939).

The best and most complete statement of the available facts about Lincoln is Carl Sandburg's magnificent six-volume work, *Abraham Lincoln: The Prairie Years* and *The War Years* (N. Y., 1926-1939).

In the history of history a myth is a once valid but now discarded version of the human story, as our now valid versions will in due course be relegated to the category of discarded myths.
—CARL BECKER: *Everyman His Own Historian*

FORMOSA (TAIWAN) HAS BEEN
very much in the news since World War II, for that is the
island off the China coast to which the Nationalist armies of
Chiang Kai Shek were driven when the Communists overran
all China on the mainland. So a good deal is known today
about Formosa. Two hundred and fifty years ago, Europe
and the United States knew very little indeed about it, and
almost literally nothing of its history, people, language.
Early in the eighteenth century this ignorance was dis-
pelled by a book, *An Historical and Geographical Description of the Island of Formosa, with an Explanation of the
Religion, Customs, and Manners of the Inhabitants.* Happily,
the book announced itself as being by George Psalmanaazaar,
"a Native of that Island." Londoners had the greatest curiosity about this hitherto unknown island, and about the
"native" who now brought his firsthand experience to add to
the world's knowledge. Their curiosity was fanned by the
fact that Psalmanaazaar, once presumed to have been a
cannibal, was now presumed to have become a Christian. It
was a pleasure-seeking, gossip-loving world of fashion, gravi-
tating between White's gambling club and the newest play

by Congreve or Wycherly. Between avid discussions of Swift's newest thrust in *The Battle of the Books* or *The Tale of a Tub*, any new sensation was eagerly welcomed. Further, Psalmanaazaar knew very well that the staunch Anglicanism of most of his readers would be tickled by his story of how the polemicists of that faith had snatched him from the vain wiles of the Jesuits. He was easily presented as a young man of noble birth, ability and good looks, "a Christian who was once by his own confession a cannibal." The fashionable world took him to its heart immediately, for the converted heathen, religious or political, is even today dear to the Anglo-Saxon heart. And so he was in the London of 1704, in which Psalmanaazaar's sensational book appeared.

The author had further endeared himself to the Bishop of London by translating the English catechism into Formosan, the alphabet and grammar of which language had been thoughtfully included in the book on Formosa. So pious a work induced the Bishop to sponsor Psalmanaazaar socially and to baptize him publicly in a glittering ceremony. Thereafter, he was wined, dined, and presented to royalty. He fascinated Dr. Johnson, whose devotion to the church and its establishment led him to a perhaps ill-merited faith in the rascally Dr. Dodd, later hanged for forgery. The acumen which enabled Johnson instantly to spot the shakiness of James Macpherson's alleged translations from the ancient Gaelic manuscripts of Ossian, was apt to desert him when religion or politics came into the Johnsonian view.

The book was immensely popular, and was immediately translated into French and German. It was full of just the kind of thing people wanted to believe about unknown islands—the people whose descendants just loved *Trader Horn* and *The Cradle of the Deep*. For Psalmanaazaar had decked out his "history" with gaudy stories about how the prophets had commanded the Formosans to burn "20,000

Hearts of Young Male Children, under nine years of Age" upon their altars. When his readers had had their appropriate thrill, and some had objected that such barbarities simply could not be true, Psalmanaazaar pointed out that the early history of other religions pictured events not much different.

Formosa was Japanese, he insisted, telling a tale of made-to-order history to support it. Meryaandanoo, a Chinese, had emigrated to Japan, he explained, and there worked his way up to a position of great trust under the Emperor. After captivating the empress with his charm, he intrigued in such a way as to bring about the death of both emperor and empress, seizing the throne of Japan for himself. He then coveted Formosa, and secured permission to send a delegation there to sacrifice to the Formosan gods. Soldiers were landed on Formosa in elephant-borne palanquins, each concealing some thirty men, but with animals for the "sacrifice" visible at the windows. The soldiers smuggled thus in "Trojan-elephant" style into the country, effected a practically bloodless conquest. Thus Meryaandanoo became Emperor of both Formosa and Japan, and for his new country he instituted laws which are described in detail.

Does it all sound ridiculous? Perhaps, but it is essentially no more so than some other historical accounts which are quite true. Most people were convinced, but soon there began to be a few criticisms, and in the following year, in the preface to a new edition, Psalmanaazaar felt obliged to answer twenty-five of them. Did his accounts differ from former ones by the Dutch historian, Candidius? Then Candidius was a liar, and if Psalmanaazaar were perpetrating a fraud, wouldn't it be easier for him to agree with former authorities, and thus get easier credence? Did his account differ from those of Dutch merchants who had called at Tyowan? Well, Tyowan and Formosa were not the same island. He had dined, he said, with Dr. Hans Sloane, Secretary to the Royal Society, Lord Pembroke, Baron Spannheim, the Prussian Ambassador, and Father Fountenay, a Jesuit scholar, and all were satisfied, he reported.

Somewhat rougher was the examination by Edmund Halley, the famous astronomer and professor of mathematics at Oxford. Did the sun shine down the chimneys in Formosa, asked Halley. Psalmanaazaar said no, but quickly caught himself and insisted that it was only because the chimneys there "do not stand perpendicular, but the Smoak is carried through the walls of the House by crooked pipes, and their ends are turn'd directly upwards, the better to convey it to the Air." Halley asked more questions, about the length of shadows at mid-day, and the length of twilight. He knew very well that Formosa was on the Tropic of Cancer, and that at certain seasons there would be vertical sun. Psalmanaazaar proved surprisingly vague in all such matters.

Then, rather suddenly, whether he felt the cold breath of exposure closing in about him, or whether he had a rush to the head of new-found Christian conscience, Psalmanaazaar confessed the whole miserable business. He had never been near Formosa and knew nothing about it at all. In fact, he had never been out of Europe. He could only regret "the base and shameful imposture of passing upon the world for a native of Formosa and a convert to Christianity, and backing it with a fictitious account of that island and of my own travels, conversion, etc., all or most of it hatched in my own brain without regard to truth or honesty."

The whole thing had been the sheerest invention. But what invention! Psalmanaazaar himself paid tribute to it when, in his second-edition attempt to vindicate himself, he had written:

" . . . for he must be a Man of prodigious parts, who can invent the Description of a Country, contrive a Religion, frame Laws and Customs, make a Language, and Letters,

etc. and these different from all other parts of the world
. . . hence the vanity of that English Gentleman, who would
needs persuade me I was his Countryman, is very plain,
for since he took it for a Forgery, he must conclude that no
body had Wit or Judgment enough for such a contrivance
but a true born Englishman."

No faker ever wrote a better tribute to his own ingenuity.
Psalmanaazaar was an artful dodger. After confessing, he
repudiated his confession, and then confessed again. And he
remained slippery to the end. Nobody ever found out with
any precision who he really was. His real name has never
been learned. It is pretty certain that he was born in southern
France, and that he had at one time posed in Rome as a
Japanese. But the real and the imaginary are so intertwined
in his life that nobody has ever entirely untangled them.
Even when he wrote a later book of memoirs purporting to
describe his real life, he never deigned to give his real name,
and few people would have believed him if he had. All that
is really known of George Psalmanaazaar is that he was a
monumental liar who spent his whole life play-acting in a
dream world and who came within an ace of getting a large
part of that world incorporated (for a time, at least) into
history.

Psalmanaazaar's own book is, of course, more entertaining than
anything that can be written about it. But there is a quite full
account of this historical faker in the *Cornhill Magazine* for May,
1879, by Henry G. Hewlitt, under the title of *Two Impostors of
the Eighteenth Century*. (The other was Ireland, the forger.)

Piltdown Man and the Cardiff Giant

HISTORY IS THE STORY OF MAN'S stay on this toilsome ball we call the earth. Most of that story is reconstructed from the consciously recorded notations about it that man has himself left behind—that is, from the written record.

But as we go back down the corridor of time some five thousand years, contemporary written records begin to fail. Yet even at the time when his own records vanish, man is seen to have been just about as he is today, physically and mentally. There are good reasons to suppose that man's story goes back long beyond the written record, and reason to suppose that he was not always as he is today, but reached his present form by a long tortuous travail through ages that make the whole recorded history seem but the yesterday of time.

The historians rather sniffishly call this "pre-history," with a distinct implication that all that has gone before the written record begins may be highly interesting, but is so speculative and based on such slippery evidence that it deserves a classification outside true history. Of course, the whole story of mankind from his veriest beginnings is his history, but the distinction remains valid—for the endless ages before writing takes up the story, we have to depend on other evidence. And that is the evidence of the fossilized remnants of the bodies of men and beasts, curiously preserved in certain places and from time to time fortuitously discovered. With them are the tools and implements and weapons and ornaments left behind, long imbedded in gravels and rocks whose relative positions can by long study be made to yield their own story and timetable.

The study of these early remains of man before he left any written record is so involved that the men who practice it, the paleontologists and archaeologists, have developed a whole science aside from the usual practices of the historian; the enforced specialization has emphasized this cleavage between "pre-history" and "history."

In the nineteenth century especially, men were fascinated by exploration of this "pre-history," for the man without specialized education hastily assumed that Darwin implied descent of man from the great apes. The more scientific view was that probably both are descended from some unknown common ancestor. But the popularization of Darwin's studies led men to seek eagerly for some "missing link" between man and ape.

No human bones have ever been found which coincide with the earliest evidence of man, which is found in "eoliths" or crudely worked implements of flint and stone. These suggest beings intelligent enough to shape crude implements as long as 500,000 years ago. Animal remains of that time are well known and plenty, but no direct trace of man at that remote period has been found.

At Trinil, Java, in 1891, there were found the remnants of a skull which, while not human, suggested some not entirely ape-like creature. It was dated from the late Pleistocene or First Ice Age, and they called it *pithecanthro-*

pus erectus, the walking ape-man. At Heidelberg, other such remains were found, progressively more nearly human and, at last, in the Neanderthal, near Duesseldorf, were found the remnants of a really human structure whose age is guessed at between 50,000 and 100,000 years. But this was distinctly a man, and there was a great gap between it, in time and development, and the Java skull.

So the world was in a receptive mood for the announcement in 1911 that there had been a great find at Piltdown, in Sussex, England, some forty-five miles south of London. Charles Dawson, a solicitor interested in an amateur way in fossils, had passed some workmen digging in brown flint of a sort which often contained fossils. He asked them to watch out for anything that looked like bones, and soon they came to him with the broken fragments of an extraordinarily thick skull. At first Dawson was only mildly interested, but at length he took the fragments to Arthur Smith Woodward of the British Museum, and Woodward joined him in a concentrated search for more fossil fragments. They were found, particularly part of a jaw-bone, and a tooth.

They were patched together, studied. The cranial fragments, though very thick and of small brain capacity, seemed distinctly human. But the jaw-bone seemed ape-like. Some scientists doubted that the two belonged together, yet the coincidence they were found close together, with no other skull parts found, made it seem that they must belong together. Sir Arthur Keith so concluded after five years of careful study, and he published his conclusions in a book, *The Antiquity of Man.* Hundreds of essays and books were published about the "Piltdown Man"; he became, in the popular mind, at least, the "first human." Hundreds of museums displayed casts of the head as reconstructed from the remains, and a generation of textbooks described it and speculated on its significance. The thick skull and the much thinner, ape-like jaw projected a creature that did not fit well into the scale that had been constructed of the rise of man, but it was all the more intriguing for that. For two generations the Piltdown Man was a star attraction of popular science.

But there was always some skepticism among scientists themselves. In 1946 Dr. Franz Weidenreich, discoverer of ancient human remains near Peking in 1928, expressed himself as skeptical of the Piltdown discoveries. With World War II, certain techniques had been developed for measuring the amount of fluorine absorbed by objects buried in the soil. These and other new tests were now applied to the Piltdown relics.

In November, 1953, came the explosion. Scientists of the British Museum and Oxford University solemnly announced that their tests had shown that the Piltdown cranium was that of an ancient man right enough, but that the jawbone on which the great age and the half ape-like appearance of the reconstructions had been based was that of a modern ape. But they went much farther:

"The faking of the mandible and canine is so extraordinarily skillful and the perpetration of the hoax appears to have been so entirely unscrupulous and inexplicable as to find no parallel in the history of paleontological discovery."

And thus the long forty-year reign of Piltdown Man ended with the ugly word "hoax." The experts hazarded no opinion as to the hoaxer, laying no specific accusation against Dawson, who had died in 1916. Dr. J. S. Weiner, who with Dr. K. P. Oakley and Prof. W. E. LeGros Clark, conducted the exposure, told the whole story in *The Piltdown Forgery* (Oxford, 1955). In 1954, further examination of the other relics and artifacts found with the Piltdown skull showed that they came from differing countries and ages; that they had been artificially stained to simulate age-weathering; that the teeth in the jaw-bone had been ground down, and that a beaver tooth imbedded in a lump of gravel had been set in a gum compound.

Thus it has been made clear that not only the written records of history, but the physical evidence of pre-history are subject to the machinations of man.

Skull-scrutiny is a tricky business at best and lends itself to skulduggery. There were at one time on exhibition in England two skulls, each avowed by the exhibitor to be that of Oliver Cromwell. One was very much smaller than the other. The exhibitor of this smaller skull, taxed with a difference which was apparent even to the casual beholder, explained that the one he was showing was the skull of Cromwell as a very small boy.

The absorbing interest which man has always showed in his early ancestry has led to numerous efforts to provide the kind of evidence that is wanted. One of the best examples, which provided a nation-wide flurry of interest and excitement, though it never fooled the experts for an instant, was the Cardiff Giant.

It was on October 18, 1869, that the newspapers of Syracuse, New York, headlined "A Wonderful Discovery," and were followed by the papers of the entire nation. Dug up on "Stub" Newell's farm near Cardiff, New York, there had emerged the massive figure of what was taken to be the fossilized body of a giant man.

The figure was 10 feet 4½ inches tall and weighed 2990 pounds. Old Onandaga Indian tales of great stone giants were revived. Prof. James Hall, director of the New York State Museum, called it (with some justice) "the most remarkable object yet brought to light in this country." Alexander McWhorter, a Yale graduate student, identified the figure with the Phoenician God Baal, and painstakingly read from one of the arms, and even translated, an "inscription" that wasn't there at all. Thousands thronged the farm to see the giant, despite the skepticism of many. There were three thousand visitors in one day, and admission money rolled in for William C. Newell and his friend, George Hull of Binghamton. Bookings were made to exhibit the giant. Barnum tried to get it and, failing to do so, had a replica made. For a time both were on exhibit at the same time in New York.

In December, only two months after the "wonder" had been unearthed, George Hull told the whole story. He was an agnostic and had become irritated by an argument over the Scriptural assurance that "there were giants in those days." He'd give them something to talk about, he thought to himself.

So Hull went to Fort Dodge, Iowa, and had a huge block of gypsum quarried. This was then sent to a Chicago stonecutter to be hewn into a very rough likeness of Hull himself. It was then treated with ink and sulphuric acid and quietly shipped to Newell's farm. Newell buried it behind the barn in 1868. Allowing a year to pass, so that any neighborhood talk of his unusual shipment might be forgotten, Newell ordered a well dug behind his barn. And the diggers came straightway on the giant.

After its day in the sun, the bulky figure lay in storage for many years, passing from one owner to another, until at last it wound up in Cooperstown, New York, where the Farmers' Museum still shows it to the curious. And Carl Carmer, an authority on upper New York State, says there are still plenty of people thereabouts who believe the Cardiff

Giant is evidence that "there were giants in the earth in those days."

The only post-exposure account in book form of the Piltdown Man is the Weiner book mentioned above. All accounts published before 1953 are, of course, no longer very helpful. The newspapers of November, 1953, all contain accounts, those in the *Illustrated London News* of November 28, 1953, and July 10, 1954, being especially well illustrated.

The Cardiff Giant is revealed in detail in New York History, Vol. XXIX, No. 3 ("The Cardiff Giant Hoax," by James Taylor Dunn). Carl Carmer tells the story in amusing style in *Listen for a Lonesome Drum* (N. Y., 1936), his volume of New York State folklore.

An up-to-date sketch of "pre-history" became available in late 1956. It is *In Search of Adam*, by Herbert Wendt, but it was not yet available as this was written.

I have ransacked a previously untouched tumulus, and in it I found, as usually happens, flint axes, bronze swords, Roman coins, and a twenty-sou piece bearing the effigy of Louis-Philippe I, King of the French.
—ANATOLE FRANCE: Preface, *Penguin Island*.

From about the year 1400 until close to the beginning of the seventeenth century, there stood in the Cathedral at Siena a bust, one of a long row of busts of the Popes. It was inscribed, simply, "John VIII, a Woman from England."

This bust is now gone to oblivion with all but the memory of a slice of history once universally believed—that a woman once sat in the chair of St. Peter. The story was unquestioningly believed both by Protestants and Catholics for hundreds of years. Now it has been completely discredited, and relegated to the lumber-room in the attic of history.

Eight hundred years after Christ, the Papacy was something quite different from what it has become. The Popes of that time were operating in a field and at a level which differed very little from those of the political leaders of the time. The succession was subject to the same political considerations, and the morality of the occupants of the Papal throne was no different than those of purely temporal rulers. Conduct which today seems scandalous was the accepted practice of rulers in the spiritual as well as the temporal realms. So the story of Pope Joan (Papissa Joanna)—the woman also known as John VIII, and at other times as Gilberta, Agnes, and Angelicus—did not seem nearly as outrageous to people who lived before the Reformation as it does to us today. It was universally accepted. And the story that was accepted was this:

Joan was a girl of English descent, born at Mainz or Ingelheim, and educated at Cologne. She was outstandingly handsome and incredibly learned and intelligent. In order to elope with a monk of Fulda with whom she had fallen in love, Joan adopted man's dress. The lovers traveled widely on the whole continent of Europe, and at length, during a stay at Athens, Joan's lover died. She then went to Rome, still in man's garb, and soon astonished clerical circles by her brilliant mind. When Pope Leo IV died, in 853, she was chosen Pope to succeed him, under the name John VIII. After functioning ably as Pope for more than two years, the story went, her imposture was revealed in a startling manner. In the course of a ceremonial procession from the Coliseum to the Church of St. Clemens the Pope suddenly gave birth to a child. Accounts vary, but she is said either to have died on the spot in shame and childbirth, or to have been stoned to death by the angry populace.

All of this, which sounds wildly fanciful, did seem to have some circumstantial backing. There was a certain street in Rome which appeared to be consistently and pointedly avoided by the Papal processions, and the rumor persisted that there a memorial column and a statue of a woman with a child in her arms had been set up. There were also certain ceremonies in the Papal enthronements connected with the use of the *sedia stercorario* which were misinterpreted as being insurance against any such misadventure happening again.

But, of course, the origin of the story was far earlier than the legends based on such stories. It was first promulgated in a book of Anastatius in 886, only thirty years after the death of Pope Leo IV. At least 150 writers during the thirteenth to sixteenth centuries repeated the story as genuine. The chief account was in Martinus Polonius, confessor to Pope Gregory X, but later students have come to believe that the Pope Joan story was inserted into his writings much later, about 1278-1312. A German miracle-play of 1480, called "The Canonization of Pope Joan," became very popular. At about the same time Higden's *Polychronicon*, written at Chester, England, and first printed by Caxton in 1495 (later revised by Treveris in 1527), had the following curious version of the story:

"After Pope Leo, Johanna English was pope for two years and five months. It is said that Johanna English was a woman and was in youth clad with her leman in men's clothes. [They went] to Athens, and learned there diverse sciences. So that thereafter she came to Rome and had there great men as scholars, and read there three years. Then she was chosen by favor of all men. And her leman brought her with child. But for she knew not her time when she should have [her] child, as she went from St. Peter's to the Church of St. John Lateran, she began to travail of child and had a child between the Colosseum and St. Clement's. Then it followeth in the story that she was buried there, and for the Pope turned there out of the way, men suppose that it is for hate of that wonder mishap. This pope is not reckoned in the book of Popes, for she was a woman and ought not to be Pope. She was born at Magounce in Almayn on the Rhine."

At about the same time, the *Nuremburg Chronicle* of 1493, the first elaborately illustrated book ever printed, not only re-told the story as fact, but presented a woodcut "portrait" of Pope Joan.

By the time Gibbon wrote the *Decline and Fall* in 1788, he was able summarily to refer to the Pope Joan story as that of "a mythical female Pope." David Blondel, a Calvinist Divine, wrote a whole book to confute the story, and its final destruction may be laid to Johann J. I. Doellinger in writing *Papstfabeln des Mittelaelters* (Munich, 1863, translated into English, 1872).

The complete refutation of the story lies in the fact that the death of Pope Leo IV has now been established definitely as having occurred July 17, 855, instead of 853. Anastatius, whose books are charged with some of the earliest accounts of Pope Joan, reported to Lothar I the immediate choice of Benedict III to succeed Leo IV. Thus there is simply no time interval in which the two-year "Papacy" of Joan could have occurred. As Anastatius died September 29, 855, knowing very well about Benedict's immediate succession to Leo, his account published thirty years later with the Pope Joan story must have been tampered with by someone else. Further, the Patriarch Photius, a contemporary who hated the Papacy and especially Benedict III, never mentions any such incident, as he surely would have done if any such thing was known at the time. The alleged "circumstantial" confirmation of the Papal processions and ceremonies have been otherwise and satisfactorily explained.

Thus nothing remains of Pope Joan, except to note that after hundreds of years with a legitimate place in history, she has now been relegated to the attic as fable, simple, even if not pure.

One of the most comprehensive accounts of Pope Joan is in *Fabel und Geschichte* by Wilhelm Edlen von Janko (Vienna, 1880), but this is not available in English. Emmanuel Royidis' "romantic biography," *Papissa Joanna*, first saw print in Greek in 1886, but is translated by Lawrence Durrell as *Pope Joan* (London, 1954). It contains more romance than biography.

Maria Monk and the Anti-Catholics

SOMETIMES, AS WE HAVE SEEN, history is made a liar. But there are other times when liars have made history. The flood of books, pamphlets, and newspaper articles that swept over the United States during the latter three-quarters of the nineteenth century in agitating the anti-foreigner and anti-Catholic movements in the name of "nativism" was plentifully tinctured with lies. For, as a cynic has observed, if you want to see man at his lowest level, observe what he does to his fellow men in the name of God.

During the Colonial era and for the first thirty years or so of the new American government, there was little feeling against immigrants or minority religious groups. There were some legal restrictions against them, but these were not oppressive in fact. In the third decade of the nineteenth century, however, immigration began to become a mass movement, and the competition of the newly-arrived for jobs began to be felt just at the time when the Catholic Church began to be visible and ubiquitous. Protestant defensive mechanisms were aroused in the religious field itself, in the political field as typified by the Know-Nothing Party, and in the press by the rise of several publications specially devoted to the alleged efforts at domination by newly-arrived groups with political and religious ties strongly influenced from abroad.

In 1830 the first "no-Popery" newspaper was established, and by 1834 sufficient feeling had been aroused to lead to the burning by a mob of the Ursuline Convent in Charleston, Massachusetts. The stage was set for the appearance of "the Uncle Tom's Cabin of the Anti-Catholic movement."

This was a lurid book, luridly entitled *The Awful Disclosures of Maria Monk*. The author of this shocker had appeared in New York in 1836 and had begun to circulate a story of spicy goings-on behind the walls of convents. The public appetite for such had been whetted by *Six Months in a Convent*, by Rebecca Theresa Reed (Boston, 1835). But Maria Monk was what the readers were waiting for. Her book sold 300,000 copies before the Civil War, a great many more afterward, and it is still selling to some extent.

Maria told a moving story of how, after a Protestant upbringing near Montreal, she entered the Hotel Dieu to be educated and to become a nun. To her horror she found the place a den of sin, with secret tunnels admitting priests to the convent for purposes whose results flowered in the strangling of unwanted babies, buried in lime pits. It was all very shocking, and just what a particular section of the public wanted. The book was apparently written by a Rev. J. J. Slocum from Maria's dictation.

It provoked an immediate reply called *Awful Exposure of the Atrocious Plot*, to which Slocum replied in turn. But the Hotel Dieu maintained silence in the face of demands for an investigation.

At length, two ministers, Rev. G. W. Perkins and W. F. Curry, were allowed to inspect the Hotel Dieu. They reported that they found no trace of the practices alleged, and that it did not even resemble the convent as described by Maria. Of course it was immediately suggested that the Hotel Dieu had been hurriedly altered to erase the evidence. Colonel William L. Stone, editor of the *New York Commercial Advertiser*, then journeyed to Montreal and was allowed to inspect the convent from cellar to garret. He, too, gave it a clean bill of health. In the meantime, Maria's mother had been located near Montreal. She reported that her daughter had always been somewhat wild and unstable as a result of a childhood injury, and had been placed in a Catholic Magdalen asylum in Montreal.

By this time, some of the more conscientious Protestant papers were beginning to repudiate the story. The *Christian Spectator*, in June, 1837, said that "If the natural history of 'gullibility' is ever written, the impostures of Maria Monk must hold a prominent place in its pages."

Before the end of the year Maria and at least two of her backers were quarreling in court over their shares of the profits from her book, and then on August 15, 1837, Maria herself disappeared. There was a hue and cry that she had been abducted, but she quickly turned up in Philadelphia at the home of a Dr. W. W. Sleigh. Here she told at least two stories, one that she had been physically abducted, another that she had been offered a large sum to accompany some priests, but had escaped and sought refuge with Dr. Sleigh, who interested himself in what appeared to be a woman in distress. After observing her for some days while she quarreled with her sponsors, Slocum and others, Dr. Sleigh wrote an *Exposure*, and gave his opinion that she was incapable of taking care of herself and should be protected.

The anti-Catholic papers which had made such good capital of Maria's story refused to concede anything, and continued on their regular way. But Maria herself gradually faded from view. The remainder of her story is clouded by rumor and lack of evidence, but it is clear that she came to a sad end, dying on New York City's Welfare Island in 1849 after a number of interludes which were neither conventual nor conventional. There seems no doubt whatever today that Maria Monk and her book were of equal frailty.

But that is not to say that they did not have a tremendous influence on the politics of the remainder of the century, or even on relations with Canada, for the whole affair raised a vast indignation in the latter country, where the Hotel Dieu was known as an old and respected institution.

And though Maria Monk passed from the scene and her book was completely discredited, a tone for controversy had been set. As the wave of Irish immigration swelled during the Civil War and failed to abate thereafter, the old controversies were revived and fanned by further falsehoods. Forgetting the regiments of staunch Irish who had fought for the Union, certain specialized newspapers and societies continued the "nativism" campaign. A horrendous "Fourth Degree Oath of the Knights of Columbus" was circulated, and the American Protective Association had its mushroom growth from 1887 to the end of the century.

Washington Gladden, one of the more enlightened Protestant Ministers, told in his *Recollections* how it touched even him:

"The movement began with the wide dissemination of literature of the most surprising character," he recalled. "The document most extensively circulated was entitled 'Instructions to the Catholics.' It purported to have been issued by the order of the Pope; the headlines generally made that assertion; the names of eight archbishops were signed to it, and the counter-sign of Cardinal Gibbons was appended. This document, in the form of a tract for general circulation, was brought to me by dozens of men,—most of whom supposed that it must be genuine. The 'Instructions to the Catholics' included such admonitions as these: 'We view with alarm the rapid spread of educated intelligence, knowing well that wherever the people are intelligent the priest and prince cannot hope to live on the labor of the masses whose brains have been fertilized by our holy catechism. . . . We view with alarm the rapid diffusion of the English language. . . .' "

It is hard to believe that this was not burlesque, but—

"The astounding fact is that this document was freely circulated for many months, and that it was published in scores of anti-Catholic papers. No exposure of its fraudulent nature, so far as I know, was made in the religious or secular newspapers."*

Gladden assures us that thousands of Americans, able to read and write, and hence presumedly educated to at least some extent, believed that high prelates of the Roman Catholic Church were stupid enough to write such a document and sign it.

The madness spread; it was freely said that Catholics were importing arms in coffins, and drilling nights in church basements; many people bought rifles to defend their homes when the storm broke.

At so explosive a moment there appeared a forged encyclical under the name of Pope Leo XIII, specifically releasing all Catholics from any oath of allegiance to the United States and giving specific orders that "on or about

* Washington Gladden, *Recollections* (Boston, 1909). Quoted by permission of Mrs. Walter R. Marvin, Headmistress, Columbus School for Girls, Columbus, Ohio.

the feast of Ignatius Loyola, in the year of the Lord 1893, it will be the duty of the faithful to exterminate all heretics found within the jurisdiction of the United States."

This rank and impudent forgery was reprinted in all anti-Catholic papers for many weeks. Gladden testifies to the admirable conduct of the Catholics under this abuse. "They endured, with great forbearance," he says, "the monstrous falsehoods which were told about them; they waited patiently for the day when the mists of suspicion and fear would clear away."

For his part in exposing these forgeries, Gladden was wildly accused of being in the pay of the Roman Catholic archbishop, and it is likely that his steadfastness lost him the presidency of Ohio State University. The hurricane of anti-Catholic billingsgate, based largely on forged documents, subsided in its most virulent form almost as quickly as it arose, yet twenty years later (and perhaps, Heaven help us, even today) some of these false tales continued to circulate.

The whole anti-Catholic agitation of the latter part of the nineteenth century is a study that can scarcely fail to bring a blush to the cheeks of any American. But it is an absorbing one. Specially apropos to this sketch are "Maria Monk and Her Influence" by Ray Allan Billington, in the *Catholic Historical Review* for October, 1936 (Vol. XXII, No. 3). Billington's *The Protestant Crusade* is also excellent. Washington Gladden's *Recollections* (Boston, 1909) is a statement by a courageous Protestant nauseated by the proceedings he had to watch. The *Colophon*, Vol. 17, has a good account, "The Maria Monk Affair," by Ralph Thompson. Written in a somewhat sardonic vein, but always interesting on this conflict, is Reuben Maury's *The Wars of the Godly*, (N. Y., 1928). A good overall view of the problem is to be found in John Higham's *Strangers in the Land: Patterns of American Nativism* (Rutgers, 1955), and Carl Wittke's *The Irish in America* (Baton Rouge, 1956) is the newest and by far the best study of the social, political, and religious problems raised by the Irish immigration to America.

I shall cheerfully bear the reproach of having descended below the dignity of history.
—MACAULAY: *History of England*, Vol. 1, Chap. 1

The Casket Letters of Mary, Queen of Scots

NEARLY EVERYBODY HAS A strong and definite feeling about Mary, Queen of Scots. Either they think of her as a cold-blooded, heartless, plotting murderess, or as a charming and somewhat wistful lady harshly dealt with by fate, by her relatives, and by history.

As always, the truth probably lies somewhere between the two extremes, and we are not going to try to find it here in a short discussion when all the historians of the past four hundred years have failed in many volumes to pin it down.

What is to be looked into here is a mystery within a mystery—the Casket Letters, on which hangs a heavy part of the evidence against Mary. To this day, it is uncertain whether the letters themselves are genuine or not. And until that is definitely decided, it will be very difficult for historians to close their books on Mary Stuart.

The casket letters are eight unsigned, undated, unaddressed letters found with a set of sonnets in a silver box, or casket, on June 20, 1567. They incriminate Mary and the Earl of Bothwell, who was shortly to become her third husband, in the murder of Lord Darnley, her second husband. The letters were discovered by political enemies of Mary

167

about four months after Darnley's murder and were produced by the rebel Scottish chiefs in 1568 at an inquiry in England called to hear charges and counter-charges against, and by, Mary. After the hearings they were taken back to Scotland, where they disappeared. They have never been seen since that day, though Queen Elizabeth herself tried in vain to get them. Only copies, represented to be accurate, exist today. But endless hours of study and ink by the quart have been spent in trying to show what, if anything, they have to tell history.

In the first place, let us remember that in the sixteenth century the succession to the crown of England was by no means as fixed and defined as it is today. Mary was the daughter of King James V of Scotland and his queen, Mary of Lorraine. She was betrothed as an infant to Henry VIII of England, but jealousies between the realms prevented the marriage, and the Scots renewed an ancient alliance with France. The child-queen, five years old, was taken to France, where, after a ten-year residence with her relatives, the Guise family, she married Francis, the Dauphin of France, in 1558, the same year in which Elizabeth I became Queen of England. To Roman Catholic Europe, Elizabeth was illegitimate, and Mary was properly Queen of England. Mary became Queen of France on Francis' accession, but in 1560 Francis died, and his widow, Mary, embarked for Scotland to assert her authority as a girl of not quite nineteen years in a land torn by strife between Catholic and Protestant parties, the former supported by France, the latter by England. On the throne of Scotland, Mary quickly proved her authority, her administrative ability, and her charm.

Mary was prospective heir to Elizabeth as the English queen, should Elizabeth die childless, and Mary proceeded to marry Henry, Lord Darnley, himself one of the claimants to the English throne after Elizabeth. But Darnley was ambitious, and armed rebellion in Scotland against Mary was succeeded by palace intrigue. Rizzio, Mary's secretary for correspondence with France, was murdered almost before her eyes in Holyrood Palace, probably with the connivance of Darnley, but Darnley protested his innocence and was reconciled with Mary. A sulky and undependable man, he became the target for further intrigue, and James Hepburn, Earl of Bothwell, the best and most dependable soldier Mary had, began to plot his exit.

While Darnley was staying at Kirk o' Field, a small estate near Edinburgh, a heavy gunpowder explosion shook the whole city, and in the ruins of Kirk o' Field the next morning the bodies of Darnley and a page boy were found near a garden wall, both strangled.

That Bothwell was directly responsible for this murder, no one doubts. The question is whether, or to what extent, Mary was jointly responsible with him for her own husband's murder. Three months later, she married Bothwell, a Protestant.

A storm of indignation swept Scotland, and within a month a rebel force compelled her abdication in favor of her son, James, who later became James I of England. She fled to England and death, to martyrdom or a well-deserved expiation, according to the point of view.

But it is with the casket letters that we are concerned. The Earl of Morton said they were found by his servants in a silver box carried by George Dalgleish, a messenger of Bothwell. If genuine, they proved the direct complicity of Mary in the murder of Darnley. They were in French, but translations into Scottish and English were appended. The originals disappeared after the hearings, as noted. Some students believe they were destroyed by James, Mary's son.

The Elizabethan commissioners gave no specific opinion about the genuineness of the documents. Mary was not allowed to inspect any of them, originals or copies.

The letters were said to have been found on June 20, 1567. On the following day they were officially inspected by the Scottish Privy Council, according to Morton. But Morton has been shown to be a highly unreliable witness, and the Council's minutes do not support him. In July the Spanish Ambassador knew of the existence of such letters, and said in a letter that one of them referred to the explosion at Kirk o' Field. But no such reference appeared in the letters as presented to the English inquiry, which suggests that there might have been some tampering with the letters between the time they were seized and their first public presentation in December, 1568, more than a year later. But, of course, the Spanish ambassador may simply have been misinformed. There is also a curious reference at a meeting of anti-Mary Scottish Lords in December, 1567, to the fact that the letters were in Mary's handwriting and signed by her. Whereas those presented at the hearings were unsigned. They are from Mary to Bothwell, telling him how she enticed Darnley to Kirk o' Field in order that the plot against him might be carried out, and how she plotted with Bothwell his "abduction" of her which preceded their marriage. Some of the letters appeared genuine beyond question, but these are ambiguous to an extent that would permit them to refer to other events, their effectiveness depending on their presentation as part of the collection.

But one long letter especially (No. 2) is conclusive if genuine. And it is either based directly on other genuine letters, or shows the work of someone who knew Mary and her mind very well indeed. Both are possible, of course, the former by rewriting genuine but innocent letters so as to make them incriminating, the latter by the connivance of such a person as her own secretary, Sir William Maitland. He is believed to have been loyal to Mary, but strange transfers of loyalty took place in the disturbed Scotland of the sixteenth century.

Lacking the original manuscripts, it has been impossible to apply the usual tests of genuineness. But careful study has shown rather clearly that the originals were in French. That would be normal if they were written by Mary, as she was not fluent in Scottish. They certainly reveal a deep and intimate knowledge of Mary's mind and of the surrounding events and circumstances. On the other hand, her enemies desperately needed evidence of this kind against her, and the circumstances of their discovery are at the least suspicious. Andrew Lang, after long study, came to the conclusion that Letter 2, especially, is "in part authentic, in part garbled."

And there the matter stands today. Because the subject is a sentimental one, and touched also by deep religious feelings, people tend to believe in this matter as their sentiments dictate. And all the labors of four hundred years have not been able to set down a final "Yea!" or "Nay!"

Anyone who is tempted to go into the details of the study of Mary, Queen of Scots, and the Casket Letters, should be warned that this is a life work and has proved such for many a man. The investigator quickly finds himself in a no-man's-land of claims and counter-claims, evidence and counter-evidence. Many books have been written about it, and one of the best is Maj. Gen. Mahon's *Mary Queen of Scots* (Cambridge, 1924), which contains some material discovered after the appearance of Andrew Lang's *Mystery of Mary Stuart* (N. Y., 1901). Mahon inclines somewhat favorably to Mary, and Sir Edward Parry, in *The Persecution of Mary Stuart* (N.Y., 1931), is frankly her defender, calling the Casket Letters "the most cowardly and unconvincing forgeries ever made use of by a syndicate of blackmailers and criminals." More dispassionate, perhaps, is *Mary, Queen of Scots —Daughter of Debate*, by Marjorie Bowen (N. Y., 1935). The *Encyclopaedia Britannica* has a good basic discussion under "Casket Letters" as a point of departure for those who want to wade deeper into these very deep waters.

Wherein I would wish that the inventions of poets and the traditions of fabulous antiquity would suffer themselves to be purged and reduced to the form of a true and historical report. . . .

—NORTH's *Plutarch* (Theseus)

The Strange Deaths of Harding, Roosevelt and Hitler

NEWSPAPER SYNDICATES SOMEtimes offer features, already prepared for insertion in any newspaper that buys them, containing a line like this: "Specially prepared for (Name Paper)." The receiving paper simply inserts its own name, thus quickly adapting the article to its own use, and giving the reader the impression that the whole thing was the product of the enterprise of the newspaper itself.

Historians have practically been offered the same device, though generally they have been reluctant to accept it. Whenever a prominent man dies, especially a statesman of the first rank, the rumor-factory starts grinding. Soon there are stories that the death took place under mysterious circumstances which the newspapers are cooperating to conceal, or perhaps even that the man is not dead at all, but has escaped.

This we have seen in our own times. *The Strange Death of President Harding* by May Dixon Thacker (N. Y., 1930) was soon followed by *The Strange Death of Franklin D. Roosevelt* by Emanuel M. Josephson (N. Y., 1948). Hitler was scarcely announced dead in the famous bunker of the

Reichskanzlei in Berlin before the rumors began to fly that he had escaped; that the body burned outside the bunker was not his at all; in fact in 1939 there had already appeared an anonymous book *The Strange Death of Adolf Hitler.* It took three years and a turn of policy to start a good, healthy rumor about Stalin, but it came in 1956—that he had shot his wife, when in 1932 it was reported that she had died after a "long illness." It was even hazarded that he was himself murdered by associates whose lives he threatened.

Let it be made quite clear that historians reject all this gossip, simply because there is no convincing evidence to bear it out. But it does present claims to be examined, such as they are, to be rejected if that seems indicated, but perhaps accepted in time if the evidence is good enough. And, in a sense, the mere circulation of such stories, if they are widely enough believed, is in itself a facet of history.

In any event, it is practically a rule that whenever a prominent person dies, rumors concerning his death arise almost instantly, and the sifting of such rumors makes work for the historians. You might almost say that history is only a rumor verified.

In the case of Harding the process was typical, even exaggerated, in a Washington already buzzing with rumor as the story gradually unfolded of an administration known to be bogged down in a muck of massive and stinking corruption. Harding was barely dead—in fact, his body had not yet reached Washington from San Francisco where he had died suddenly in a hotel room, when the rumors began to sweep the capital; rumors that the President had ended a life which faced exposure, perhaps impeachment; rumors that perhaps his own wife, or his own personal physician, had speeded his design. The rumors were augmented because of certain small inconsistencies and confusions in the early press reports.

The President had been on an ocean voyage to Alaska, "a voyage of understanding" in the course of which he was to send up trial balloons looking toward a second term. He went through an arduous speaking schedule, and the voyage to Alaska did not rest him as had been expected. He was evidently perturbed by a secret visit from Mrs. Fall, wife of the Secretary of the Interior, and by a long code message brought to the ship by airplane. At Seattle it was cruelly hot, and the President insisted against advice on making a scheduled speech. In the early morning hours he suffered what his old friend, Surgeon-General Charles E. Sawyer, disgnosed as an attack of acute indigestion, caused, it was said, by eating crab meat. But no crab meat was on the menu, and no other member of the party was affected. The President seemed to be improving, and Dr. Sawyer issued optimistic statements. But the President could sleep only with difficulty and only in a semi-sitting posture, which had been true for some time. When the party, speeches canceled, reached San Francisco, Harding declined a suggested wheel chair, but he looked old, worn, and tired. His physicians put him to bed at the Palace Hotel. Pneumonia set in.

Though the patient rallied and seemed to be winning the fight with pneumonia, heart specialists Dr. Charles Minor Cooper and Dr. Ray Lyman Wilbur, President of Stanford University, were called in. On Wednesday, August 1, Dr. Sawyer announced that the crisis had passed.

At about half-past seven on the evening of August 3, Mrs. Harding was reading to the President agreeable words about himself by Samuel G. Blythe in the *Saturday Evening Post*. The President seemed pleased. Then quite suddenly, a tremor passed through his body, and he was dead. Mrs. Harding called for help, and doctors and nurses promptly responded. Five doctors—Sawyer, Wilbur, Cooper, Commander Boone of the Navy, and Secretary Work, who was a physician—all signed the death certificate. Though some of the doctors urged an autopsy, Mrs. Harding would not permit it, nor would she permit the usual death-mask to be made. There were varying reports of the exact time of death and of who was present.

It was quite enough. Though very little was printed, rumors swept the country that there was something mysterious about the President's death. Such rumors will not down, and even in later years, writers of the stature of Frederick Lewis Allen, Oswald Garrison Villard, and James Truslow Adams have been among those who felt that the matter would stand a good deal of clarifying. In 1930 came a book, *The Strange Death of President Harding*, by May Dixon Thacker (whose brother, Rev. Thomas N. Dixon, later ghost-wrote Harry M. Daugherty's *The Inside Story of the Harding Tragedy*). The Thacker book was presented as being based on diaries of Gaston B. Means, a former FBI operative and private sleuth who had just been released from Atlanta Penitentiary on conviction of bribery in connection with liquor release permits (and who later died there after another conviction, this time for defrauding Mrs. E. B. McLean in selling to her faked clues to the Lindbergh kidnaping).

The Means-Thacker opus is an unspeakable performance. It reads as though it had been written by Penrod Schofield. And Means had long before amply proved his complete untrustworthiness in any matter at all. But the book, with its direct innuendo that Mrs. Harding had poisoned her husband because of jealousy of the Nan Britton who claimed to be the mother of Harding's child, was widely circulated. It added much to the rumors, little to the evidence, in the case.

In fact, it is from the surrounding climate of circumstances that any "mystery" surrounding the death of Harding has arisen, not from evidence. A careful statement of the circumstances was made by Dr. Ray Lyman Wilbur in the *Saturday Evening Post* of October 13, 1923. Dr. Wilbur was on the scene, and his personal and professional reputation are beyond any reasonable question. In this article, "The Last Illness of a Calm Man," Dr. Wilbur gave the information, little known until then, that "all through the last months he [Harding] knew his physical danger. He had had symptoms that all men know mean something serious; his physicians had warned him. . . ." Dr. Wilbur's further account is not very circumstantial, but it is the expert and reliable testimony of an eyewitness. And as Samuel Hopkins Adams points out in *Incredible Era*, it is very hard to believe that there could have been a collusion to hide unpleasant truths participated in at once by men like Wilbur, Cooper, Boone, Work, and Sawyer—all of whom signed the death certificate. Even if it were conceivable that Sawyer, with his close family connections, might have done so, it seems virtually impossible that all the others would have joined in attesting the report. Dr. Sawyer, by the way, died soon afterward in a manner almost exactly duplicating the President's death, including the presence of Mrs. Harding.

The poison theory cannot, of course, be specifically disproved, since there was no autopsy. But natural death is so well borne out by the medical history and the circumstances that there remains no reasonable doubt. Even on inauguration day, Colonel Starling, the Secret Service man so long attached to President Wilson, noted Harding's "high stomach" pressing against the breast-bone. He was always troubled with "indigestion," so much so that stories of his drinking were exaggerated—even a few drinks were dearly paid for in later distress. For nearly a year he had been unable to sleep well, and then only when propped up on high pillows. The "indigestion" attack at Seattle sounds very much like bad diagnosis on Sawyer's part (he had the least impressive professional qualifications of any of the attending physicians), as certain forms of heart disease produce symptoms often mistaken for "indigestion." The strain of the mounting scandals, the dawning realization that he had placed naive trust in scoundrels who had let him down, the strain of inadvised speaking in brutal hot sun, the added strain of throwing off the pneumonia attack—all these are sufficient background for a cardiac seizure. The suddenness of death is also characteristic, and while it is true that certain poisons would produce the same result, most of such toxics leave traces which would be evident even without a post-mortem.

Thus, except for the rumor-mongers, there need never have been any suspicion about the Harding death at all, and history properly rejects all such rumors, at least until some real evidence is produced.

The death of Franklin Delano Roosevelt is parallel. That a man of sixty-three should die suddenly after twelve years of bearing the most crushing burdens of responsibility that ever fell on one man's shoulders is not a thing that seems in itself inordinately suspicious. But in this case the rumors about the President's health which had circulated widely during the preceding year or two now blossomed into the suggestion that there were mysterious circumstances surrounding his death.

The circumstances were these:

The President had returned from the Yalta Conference, during which he traveled fourteen thousand miles and went through a grueling series of conferences and entertainments. One of his first tasks was to drive through the sleet and rain to Arlington Cemetery to attend the burial of his close companion and aide, "Pa" Watson. At noon he went to the Capitol to report to Congress on Yalta. Having heard rumors of his illness, he took pains to say to the people, "I am returning . . . refreshed and inspired. I was well the entire time. I was not ill for a second until I arrived back in Washington. . . ."

But to Vice-Admiral Ross T. McIntire, Surgeon-General of the Navy, who had attended him daily since 1933, it was apparent that the President was tired. His weight was fifteen pounds below normal. McIntire insisted that the President lighten his load, take better care of himself, in preparation for the San Francisco Conference for the organization of the United Nations. Roosevelt agreed, reluctantly, to go to Warm Springs for a rest in preparation for San Francisco. There he seemed happy and more relaxed, and promptly put on eight pounds. He planned to return to Washington on April 20. On April 12, at about 1:20 P.M., he was sitting for a portrait being painted by Mrs. Elizabeth Shoumatoff, an artist who had done his portrait once before. Suddenly the President complained of "a terrible headache" and collapsed.

Commander Bruenn, who had attended the President for two years, was almost instantly at hand. But restorative measures failed, and within two hours the President was dead. Dr. James Paullin, arriving from Atlanta just before death came, concurred in Dr. Bruenn's verdict that death had been due to "a massive intracerebral hemorrhage."

The book referred to above, which summarizes all the.

whispers and rumors which immediately arose, appeared in 1948. It is a violent attack on Roosevelt and his administration, only a single chapter being devoted to the subject indicated by the title. Enough suggestions are made to kill off a half-dozen men—that Roosevelt had had minor apoplectic strokes as early as 1937—that at Teheran he was poisoned by the Russians with some slow Oriental poison handed down from the days of Genghis Kan—that the moles or wens removed by surgery suggested cancer—that his body turned black as in cases of arsenic poisoning—that on his return from Yalta he again showed signs of having been poisoned, and that the sudden death of "Pa" Watson on the journey is suspicious—that photographs of Roosevelt in 1944 were not his own but those of a "stand-in" who really functioned for him during that year—that several mysterious persons unmentioned in press reports were present when he died at Warm Springs—that the fact that there was no autopsy is suspicious—that the coffin was never opened for public view—that regular physical checkups were either not given or not honestly reported to the public.

If this is the strongest case that can be made in favor of mystery surrounding the death of FDR, serious historians need not waste much time on it. For McIntire has written a quite circumstantial account of President Roosevelt's health in *White House Physician*, in which all these rumors are categorically denied and the results of frequent successive checkups given in some detail. McIntire reiterates that the President's health was organically excellent for a man of his age; that he probably hastened his death by overwork and refusal to rest, relax and exercise as prescribed; and that the cause of death, cerebral hemorrhage, is one which heralds itself by no signs that are subject to diagnosis. Either the general rumors about President Roosevelt's ill health are quite unfounded, or McIntire is a monumental and official liar—a thing that there is no reason at all to believe, and excellent reason to disbelieve.

McIntire was not, however, present at the actual death of Roosevelt and his testimony does not apply there. But the testimony of all those who were present at Warm Springs is united in affirming that no one was present who was not well known to them all. There is no evidence of the alleged presence of suspicious persons. The President was feeling so much improved that he had planned to attend a barbecue late that afternoon. The attending physicians, on hand within minutes, were of unquestioned competence and reliability. The fact that the coffin was never opened and placed on public view has been explained by Mrs. Roosevelt herself—she says that when she and her husband had seen the custom observed in state funerals at the Capitol, with long queues filing by an open casket, they both found the idea disagreeable, and it was understood between them that they would not follow it. The simple service and the burial in the rose garden at Hyde Park had all been prescribed by the President himself in a memorandum dictated years before. There was nothing abnormal about the whole proceeding, and the rumor-mongers bear the responsibility of proving their case, which they have not even approached doing.

In the matter of the *Strange Death of Adolf Hitler*, the anonymous author makes practically no effort to substantiate a tale so wild and so devoid of supporting evidence that it stands alone even in this group of historical pariahs. No serious historian has given the thesis of this book a second thought, let alone accept the book as serious evidence of the thesis. It is, briefly, this: that about 1933 Hitler began training several "doubles" to replace him and simulate his "presence" at certain public occasions. One of these, Maximilian Bauer, permanently replaced Hitler when the Fuehrer died of poisoning at a banquet just the night before the Munich Agreement, Sept. 29, 1938, and the Hitler of history from that day on was really Bauer, impersonating the Fuehrer and carrying out the policies of the inner circle of the Nazi Party.

The anonymous author of the book is represented to be Bauer himself, who had sent the manuscript through Switzerland to a Frenchman in Nice, one Michel Simon, known through his mother to Bauer. Simon showed it to a friend who had put in with a German merchant ship, hoping to have the German translated, but there was no time, and the German merchant officer took the manuscript with him. On the transatlantic voyage he translated half of it enough to convince the publishers that they should rush it into print, which they did.

Strange enough, in all conscience. But no stranger than the stories that have been told since World War II by travelers returning from far corners of the world with stories that Hitler had been seen in Buenos Aires, in Bolivia, in Japan. Yet such stories have scarcely reached a scale of detail or dramatics which might have been expected in the case of a man who had become head of a cult of zealots. One reason is that Allied Occupation authorities took some pains to prevent the development of "shrines" to the Fuehrer's memory, to run down and scotch instantly and publicly all such rumors of an "escape." They promptly ordered as thorough an investigation into his death as was possible under the circumstances. The death took place while the Russians were capturing Berlin on April 30, 1945, and Allied officers were not able to make a complete investigation until more than three months later. When made, however, it was quite convincing. (See note at end of chapter.)

❦

Nobody has yet written a *Strange Death of Josef Stalin*, but it is probably on its way. When at last, after eleven weeks' delay, a partial text of Nikita S. Krushchev's denunciation of Stalin reached the United States (it was delivered Feb. 24-25, 1956, to a secret meeting of party faithful in Moscow and was only received in the United States, and then in an incomplete text, on June 6), its assertion that some of the surviving Russian leaders were in daily terror for their lives gave a vague suggestion that Stalin might have been murdered by one of them to save his own life. And another rumor-mill became a going concern.

Trotsky, who in later years became a historian and wrote an absorbing history of the Russian Revolution, also wrote a life of Stalin in 1941. In it he suggests strongly that Lenin in his last days, in terrible pain from arteriosclerosis with repeated "strokes," asked his close associates for poison with which he might ease his passing when he felt it to be inevitable. They all refused, says Trotsky, except Stalin, and he strongly suggests that Stalin smilingly procured for Lenin the desired poison. But, of course, Trotsky was a bitter political opponent of Stalin, and his account is scarcely to be considered impartial. The death of Stalin will never be shown to be any more mysterious than that of Trotsky, his opponent, and the Russian change of front on Stalin may yet solve the mystery of Trotsky's death. For it was freely said at the time that Trotsky was murdered at Stalin's behest. If that should be true, it may at any time seem desirable to those in charge of Russia to substantiate it.

Trotsky, banished from Russia by Stalin, took refuge in various places, winding up in a villa in Coyoacan, a suburb of Mexico City. There he fortified himself and surrounded himself by "Trotskyite" guards, some of them Americans, for he insisted that he was hounded by Stalinite agents who had already killed his son in Paris.

There seemed some ground for his suspicions, for on May 24, 1940, a gang of assailants riddled the villa with machine-gun bullets, though Trotsky and his wife escaped unhurt. Soon afterward a man who evidently satisfied the Trotskys that he was a political sympathizer began to frequent the villa. On the morning of August 20, he called and asked to show Trotsky a manuscript. They went to his study. A moment later there was a scream, and when his guards rushed to the study, they found Trotsky dying, his head brutally beaten in with a short-handled mountain-climber's pickax.

There was no mystery at all about the murder. But who was the murderer? He was convicted in 1943 and sentenced to twenty years in prison. He was installed, not in a cell, but in rooms where he lived comfortably and enjoyed many luxuries brought in to him through his attorney. Who was providing the money? Who was behind the assassin? No one has ever found out. Not even his name has been learned with precision in the thirteen years of his imprisonment. He has been variously called Mercader, alias Jacson, alias Mornard, and so on—a multiplicity of names unusual even in the midst of a conspiratorial world where aliases were the rule. The Russian press was significantly reticent, contenting itself with a few lines and indicating that the assassination was the work of "a discontented Trotskyite." After long examination, Mexican authorities generally agree that the assassin's name is Mercader, a Catalan professional Communist. But as the time for his possible release draws near, there may yet be a final chapter written which will explain who was really behind the murder of Trotsky.

Russian history since 1917 has, of course, been a great *terra incognita*, for outside historians have no access to the records, and native historians have had to do all their writing under the prescriptions of a ruling party. All of them grew up under conditions of conspiratorial secrecy. Lenin, Stalin, Trotsky—the last chapters have not yet been written.

***

Another "strange death," which remains somewhat mysterious to many people after the passage of forty years, is that of Earl Kitchener, head of the British War Office in the first years of World War I. In the spring of 1916, it was decided that Kitchener should go to Russia, to place at the disposal of the chaotic Russian War Office the experience of Britain's most distinguished soldier. The whole plan was kept highly secret; not even some of Kitchener's close friends and associates knew of it.

On June 5, Kitchener entrained at King's Cross Station for Scapa Flow. The messenger who was to bring his ciphers and codes to the station failed to show up, a not very reassuring portent, but the party took the train anyway. Kitchener had lunch with Admiral Sir John Jellicoe aboard the *Iron Duke* at Scapa Flow, and the Admiral personally chose the course to Archangel, the destination of the Cruiser *Hampshire*, which was to carry the Kitchener party. A heavy northeaster was blowing, and a course hugging the west shores of the Orkneys was chosen from three alternatives, as being in the lee of the storm, thus making it easier for the destroyer escort. German mines had not been found so far north, and the passage had been safely used by other craft a short time before. Jellicoe took full responsibility for the course.

Kitchener boarded the *Hampshire* and she set out. By 7:00 P.M. the weather had become so rough that Captain H. J. Savill of the *Hampshire* ordered the two accompanying destroyers to break off. The rough seas made mine-sweeping impossible, but it was thought they would also eliminate any possibility of attack by U-boats. At about 7:40 P.M. a terrific explosion tore the whole midsection out of the ship, and in less than ten minutes the *Hampshire* sank like a stone.

She was only a mile and a half from shore—a wild, cliff-hung coast, and the disaster was seen from shore and reported before 8:00 P.M. The ships which rushed to the rescue were able to save only twelve lives. Kitchener was not among them. His body was never found.

Naval investigations were later to show that the *Hampshire* was sunk by a mine, one of a field sowed by a German submarine not long before the *Hampshire*'s sailing, in an area never mined before by either side.

When the news reached England, rumors swept across the country like a field-fire: The secret sailing had been tipped to spies; a submarine had lain in wait; Kitchener was a prisoner of the Germans. The proof? The news of his "strange death" had been announced in Germany before the English papers appeared with it. How was this possible if there had not been a "leak"?

This odd circumstance was not explained until 1920, when Rear Admiral Sir Douglas Brownrigg's *Indiscretions of the Naval Censor* appeared. Brownrigg told that his office had released the story to the news agencies and newspapers before 12:00 noon on the sixth. But just after it had been sent out, the Admiralty received further details, and asked Brownrigg to hold up his dispatch. It was too late. It had been received by the news agencies and relayed abroad.

Brownrigg was able only to hold up the special editions of the London papers. While he was delaying the English extras, the news was published abroad, giving rise to the rumors about a leak. But even this logical explanation never quite downed the whispers which are still heard about what was at the least a series of unhappy errors in judgment which led to the "strange death" of Britain's first soldier.

Aside from the specific books noted above as concerned with the "strange deaths" of politically-prominent figures, there are good accounts of the Kitchener death in *The Grand Fleet*, by Admiral Viscount Jellicoe (N. Y., 1919), and the *Life of Lord Kitchener*, by Sir George Arthur (N. Y., 1920). *The Tragedy of Lord Kitchener*, by Reginald Viscount Esher (London, 1921), bases its claim to tragic elements not at all in the death, for which it holds no one to blame, but on other circumstances. The one complete account (up to 1950) of the Trotsky death investigation is *Murder in Mexico* by General Sanchez Salazar (London, 1950). Salazar is former chief of the Mexican secret police and was actively in charge of investigations when Trotsky was killed.

When it became possible for Allied soldiers to go to Berlin after the end of World War II in the European Theatre, one of those who went most eagerly was H. R. Trevor-Roper, a British intelligence officer. He was charged with learning all that happened during the last few days of the twilight of such gods as the Nazi "Third Reich" had produced, including of course the exact manner of the death of Hitler. His book, *The Last Days of Hitler*, is an excellent account of these events, and it leaves little doubt in the mind of any reasonable person that Hitler is dead.

Incidentally, one John Smith Dye, in 1864, wrote a book called *The Adder's Den*, in which he essayed to prove that President W. H. Harrison was assassinated to make way for Tyler and the annexation of Texas, and that Taylor was similarly made way with to open the way to Fillmore and thus prevent statehood for California, etc., etc.

Woodrow Wilson's Sunrise Conference

IF IT CAN BE SHOWN THAT AN American President deliberately led a reluctant people into war for selfish reasons and against their will, that is a matter of first importance. History could concern itself with no graver problem.

Every war brings reappraisal in its wake, and properly so. Hence the forty-year trail of "The Sunrise Conference."

The story is that in the early spring of 1916, *months before* the re-election campaign in which his managers placed him before the people with the slogan "He Kept Us Out of War," Woodrow Wilson held a secret early-morning conference at the White House with Congressional leaders in which he revealed himself as eager for war and anxious to surmount their opposition to any such course. If this is true, it calls for a complete revision of the canonical view of Wilson, and is full of significance not only for the country's history but for its future.

Long months of controversy with both belligerents about infringement of various rights of neutrals had worn tempers to an edge. There was widespread criticism of Wilson as being a mere "note-writer," unable to make a firm stand in the face of repeated violations of American rights. There was also a strong body of feeling that only a firmly-continued neutrality would serve American interests and, in the long run, those of the world. There were, within the government itself, two views—that of Secretary Lansing and Ambassador Page, for instance, insisting on a showdown with Germany—and that of Secretary Bryan (who resigned rather than take even a chance of war), and of Claude Kitchin, Democratic leader in the House, who believed war would be a tragic mistake. Somewhere between these poles stood President Wilson.

The rumor spread through Washington even at the time, that a mysterious conference had been held at the White House with Congressional leaders, held in the early morning so that newsmen would not catch wind of it. The story went 'round that Wilson had pounded the table and demanded war, to the horror of the pacific Congressmen. The only persons present were presumed to have been the President, Speaker Champ Clark of the House, Rep. Kitchin, and Rep. Flood, Chairman of the Foreign Relations Committee.

The question remained unsettled until after the war itself, and most historians of the period, like Charles Beard and Hartley Grattan, felt there was no evidence of such a conference warranting its inclusion in history, though Harry Elmer Barnes credited it. In 1921, Gilson Gardner, Scripps-Howard correspondent in Washington during the war, began to probe into the story. He wrote to Kitchin, asking confirmation, as by that time Clark and Flood were dead, and Wilson a secluded invalid. Kitchin, himself suffering from a stroke, replied that such a conference had been held, and promised to discuss it later, but he gave no details. Gardner wrote an article called "Why We Delayed Entering the War" (*McNaught's Monthly*, June, 1925), publicly reopening the controversy by affirming that the "Sunrise Conference" had indeed been held, but giving little of the substance of the discussion.

Placing the time no more specifically than "the spring of 1916," Gardner sums up the discussion by saying that Wilson "informed his visitors that the time had come for the United States to get into the war." Correspondence with others supposed to have knowledge of the affair led Gardner to add that they declared that Wilson felt that a declaration of war at that time would make it unnecessary to send troops overseas at all; that Germany would be so overwhelmed at such a declaration that it would quit at once.

Gardner, on a roving assignment for E. W. Scripps in Washington throughout World War I, was highly unsympathetic to the war, and he concluded that Wilson had for some mysterious reason become "war-minded a hundred per cent," and was from June, 1917, until his death "a hard, unhuman, unrelenting Wilson."

While Gardner did a great deal toward establishing the fact of the Sunrise Conference, he was able to gather little of the exact substance of the discussions and of precisely what was said by Wilson and the others. His obvious irritation with the President was perhaps aggravated by the fact that despite his personal views of the war, his own (Scripps) papers were a material factor in re-electing Wilson in 1916, especially in carrying Ohio, normally Republican.

But to Alex Mathews Arnett, who was writing a biography of Kitchin, the matter was vital, for Kitchin had incurred considerable unpopularity for his opposition to going to war in 1916-17, and the conference tended to justify Kitchin as a restraining influence on Wilson's alleged rashness. Arnett made the most thorough investigation yet done, and announced his results in *Claude Kitchin and the Wilson War Policies* (Boston, 1937). Arnett established with considerable authenticity that such a conference actually was held at about 7:30 in the morning, so that the Congressmen could enter and leave the White House unnoticed by the press.

But unfortunately Kitchin had left no diaries or permanent records of the conference. He affirmed that it took place, but left it by no means clear whether the meeting was in February or April, a point which makes considerable difference, for in April the situation had been aggravated by the sinking on March 24 by a U-boat of the unarmed French channel steamer *Sussex*, with the loss of many lives, including Americans. Kitchin recalled that there had been a similar conference at the White House the afternoon before, including Senator Kern, Democratic leader in the Senate, and Senator Stone. Kitchin said that he, Flood, and Clark had often discussed the "Sunrise Conference" and were in agreement as to what had been said, but he regretted that they had never made a memorandum on it, as perhaps they should have done, signed by all three, with a copy for each. But no such record was made, nor did Arnett find any more circumstantial information in Kitchin's papers.

Flood was quoted by E. Yates Webb as having said that Wilson felt sure war would mean nothing more than sending a few ships, which would shorten the conflict. But Allan L. Benson, journalist and Socialist candidate for the Presidency in 1916, told Arnett that Kitchin told him about the conference the same day it happened, and said Kitchin confirmed that Wilson pounded on the table and said that if the United States entered the war promptly the whole thing would be over by August. Benson was an ardent proponent of a popular referendum on declarations of war, and may perhaps have been influenced somewhat by his strong beliefs.

Josephus Daniels' Memoirs, *The Wilson Era* (Chapel Hill, 1944), tell a somewhat different story. Daniels agrees that the Sunrise Conference was a fact and says flatly that it took place February 25, 1916. Daniels says Kitchin discussed the meeting with him shortly after it happened, and that he said Wilson's attitude was that if Germany continued as she was doing, war would come to the U. S. A. and that this might even be a good thing, as it would shorten the war as a whole. Daniels thinks Kitchin simply misinterpreted as belligerency Wilson's indignation at German tactics and his growing acceptance of a course that was becoming inevitable. Daniels then quotes Flood as having said that Wilson never said anything to the effect that war with Germany might not be a bad thing, and that Wilson himself specifically denied saying anything of the sort. This contrasts oddly with other witnesses who say they talked to Flood directly after the conference, and that Flood seemed convinced that Wilson had revealed himself as "hell-bent for war." William Allen White, in his *Woodrow Wilson* (Boston, 1925), says there was such a conference, but thinks it was in May.

There the matter stands today. It has taken nearly forty years to show that such a "Sunrise Conference" was actually held. But the fragmentary and second or third-hand reports of what was said leave considerable doubt as to precisely what was Wilson's mood. It seems quite clear that he was tired and discouraged with the long fruitless bickering with Germany, and was facing the fact that if circumstances did not mend, the United States might be drawn into war; it seems likely that he speculated on the possible advantages of "now," if it had to be "inevitably, later." But no determined or unswerving bellicosity on Wilson's part has been clearly shown, especially when read against several strong efforts by him to preserve effective neutrality between February, 1916, and April, 1917. If Wilson was a hypocrite who went to the country with peaceful slogans while nursing war in his heart, the long investigation into the "Sunrise Conference" has not shown it beyond cavil.

Gilson Gardner's investigation into the "Sunrise Conference" is described in *Lusty Scripps* (N.Y., 1932) and was reproduced by Harry Elmer Barnes in his *Genesis of the World War*. The books of Arnett and Daniels are noted in the text above. Every biography of Wilson from that of Ray Stannard Baker on down has necessarily concerned itself with the conversion of Wilson the pacifist into Wilson the war leader.

Summary execution of all history professors in America would, indeed, prevent them from doing any more bad teaching, but it would not prevent bad teaching; for time and circumstance, manners and customs, tradition and prejudice, all teach history and teach it badly. The professors, indeed, are our only correctives; their instruction is open to criticism, certainly, but at least they have made some effort to adjust it to reality, and without them we could have no anchor or mooring-line at all.

—GERALD W. JOHNSON: *American Heroes and Hero-Worship*

The Story of the Lost Dauphin and Marshal Ney

THE EVERGREEN THEME OF mystery connected with the death of men in high place has produced two perennial stories that have been knocking at the door of history for a hundred years. Historians have refused to admit them, but they still stand wistfully outside the door, refusing to be gone.

One is the story that the son and heir of Louis XVI of France did not die in a foul prison as reported, but was spirited away and appeared in America as Eleazar Williams, the "Lost Dauphin." And there is another that Marshal Ney, Napoleon's "bravest of the brave," did not die before a firing squad, but was rescued and lived out his life as an American schoolteacher, Peter Stuart Ney. They are the kind of stories that people love to believe, with death cheated and life affirmed.

In the midst of all the thunderous events of the French Revolution, it is not surprising that little attention was paid to what happened to a ten-year-old boy, even though his name was Louis Charles and his title, Duke of Normandy. But he was the son of Louis XVI and Marie Antoinette, and when his elder brother died only a few weeks before the fall of the Bastille, he had become Dauphin of France.

The Tuileries was taken, and the royal family imprisoned, together at first, but then, as Louis and his queen went to their deaths, the boy was confined separately in the tower of the Temple. The Revolution, which demanded the lives of the parents, had not even a quick death for "the little Capet"—only neglect, and confinement in a foul and filthy hole of a room, under callously cruel jailers. Under such conditions, the child's health, both physical and mental, was grievously affected.

A year later, with the fall of Robespierre, some committee remembered the child, and his prison conditions were slightly bettered, but it was too late. He was emaciated, covered with sores and tumors, as inarticulate as an animal. On the sixth of May, 1795, a physician was at last allowed to examine him. This was P. J. Desault, a competent practitioner who had served the royal family. Desault attended the child until May 30 and gave hope that proper care would bring about his recovery. But then Desault himself died suddenly and mysteriously and there were rumors that he had been poisoned. For five days there was no word from the tower room. Then two more physicians, who had never seen the Dauphin, were summoned. Three days later the boy in the Temple was reported dead. An autopsy was performed, the physicians certifying that they were "confronted with the body of a boy of about ten years old, which the commissioners represented to be that of the deceased Louis Capet." While that seems to insist rather strongly that the examining physicians were not sure of the identity of the body, it was also the usual formula of such documents of the time, and may not be significant. The child's body was buried in Ste. Margaret Cemetery. No stone was set to mark the grave.

Even at the time, these highly irregular circumstances were noted. The physicians who certified death and performed the autopsy did not know the Dauphin by sight. Was the child they attended the Dauphin at all? It is also known that the temporary commissioner of the prison, one M. Bellanger, an artist and a protege of the Duc de Provence, spent the whole day of May 31 in the prisoner's company. There remains always a possibility that Bellanger arranged to smuggle the Dauphin away and substitute another dying child.

So, at least, many people believed, and thereafter some thirty or forty people have turned up at various times and places claiming to be the Dauphin. One was the Compte de Richemont; one was Charles William Naundorff, a Prussian locksmith whose descendants even sued the French government (vainly) for the Dauphin's estate; and yet another was Eleazar Williams.

In February, 1853, America was much startled by an article in *Putnam's Monthly*, "Have We a Bourbon Among Us?" by John H. Hanson. Hanson's article told a wonderful story. The Prince de Joinville, third son of the Louis Philippe who had ascended the French throne eleven years earlier, had come to New York. There, according to the Hanson narrative, he had made diligent inquiry for one Eleazar Williams, known in northern New York State as a half-breed missionary among the Indians. When the Prince's boat, in the course of a Great Lakes trip following the route of Marquette, put in at Mackinac, Eleazar Williams was waiting on the dock. He went aboard the boat as it left for Green Bay, Wisconsin, and while aboard and later in Green Bay, there were long private conferences between the Prince and the Indian missionary. Hanson's thesis was that Joinville told Williams of his heritage and tried to get him to sign an abdication in favor of Louis Philippe. He refused, says Hanson, but some time later there arrived for Williams, as a gift of Louis Philippe, a shipment of books and a portrait by

Ingres of an unidentified man. The picture is still in the Green Bay Public Museum.

Williams apparently at first kept silence, but in 1848 there was reported in the New Orleans newspapers the death of a Frenchman named Bellanger, who gave a deathbed statement that he had brought the Dauphin to America and placed him among the Indians of northern New York state. It was this story that put Hanson on the trail. He looked up Williams, spent several years in searching for evidence, and the magazine articles were the result.

Copies were sent to Joinville, and brought an immediate denial. Joinville insisted that the meeting with Williams was entirely accidental, and the conversations casual. Hanson found quite convincing evidence, however, that Joinville had specifically inquired in New York about Williams. The deathbed confession of Bellanger is important if true, but a copy of Bellanger's "confession" was later found in Williams' handwriting, and it is possible that he invented it and got it published in the New Orleans newspaper. In 1872, a Colonel H. E. Eastman, once mayor of Green Bay, stated that he had invented the whole Williams story as a hoax, and that Williams had taken the idea from him. Yet it is odd that Eastman said nothing at the time Hanson's article appeared, but only made his claim seventeen years later, when both Williams and Hanson were dead.

The controversy was a lively one for many years. Williams was given a parish at Hogansburg, New York, and his admirers and believers in his story built him a house there. He died at Hogansburg August 28, 1858.

The whole matter lay dormant during the remainder of the century, but between 1893 and 1921, several books and many articles were published about it. Elaborate comparisons of pictures of Williams and Louis XVI and XVIII were made, proving nothing but that Williams looked a little like the Frenchmen. Williams at one time appealed to Congress to support his French claims and perhaps get him a pension, but Congress refused to act.

Eleazar Williams had a remarkable career by any standard. Even if he was not the lost Dauphin, his life repays study. He passed as the adopted son of Thomas Williams, and he certainly did not look anything like the rest of Williams' children. He always maintained that he remembered nothing of his childhood years, and those who knew him as a small boy considered him almost imbecile at that time. That is what would have been expected if he had been the boy Dauphin brought out from France in 1795, for it agrees with the child's condition after his imprisonment. The boy's physical health rapidly improved under outdoor conditions. When he was about fourteen, he was swimming at Lake George and dived into a hidden underwater rock. The resulting blow appeared the starting-point of a restored brain. Even those who question the efficacy of such therapeutics admit that it has happened, though perhaps it has happened more often in fiction than in real life.

He was given some schooling, leading to appointment as a lay missionary and teacher. As such, he became an honorary chief of the Iroquois under the name of *Onwarenhiiaki*. His close relationships with that tribe enabled him to be of great help to the American cause during the War of 1812 and to render services for which the government paid him well. He helped solve the difficult problem of removing the last of the New York State Indians to a reservation in Wisconsin, a difficult diplomatic mission which required great tact and ability. He married Madeline Jourdan, the daughter of a half-breed Indian. In 1826 he became a deacon of the Episcopal Church and did good service in and around Green Bay, Wisconsin, where he was a large land-holder. The life which trailed off to a somewhat undistinguished end at Hogansburg was, after all, a creditable and serviceable one.

Was it also that of an impostor? Or was he really the Lost Dauphin of France, in reality its king under the style of Louis XVII? History simply closes the door against the wilderness legend. It says, "This is unproved." It cannot say, "This is impossible."

History likewise accepts that Marshal Ney, the last Frenchman across the Niemen in the disastrous retreat from Moscow and Napoleon's "bravest of the brave," was stood before a wall in Paris' Luxembourg Gardens and shot by order of Louis XVIII. Yet here again a story continues to haunt the halls of history—a story that Marshal Ney cheated death and lived out a long life in America as a simple schoolteacher in North Carolina.

Whether or not Marshal Ney actually led two lives, he certainly has two tombstones. In the Pere la Chaise Cemetery at Paris there is a stone slab engraved simply "Ney." And in the little cemetery of the Third Creek Presbyterian Church near Salisbury, Rowan County, North Carolina, there is another "In Memory of Peter Stuart Ney, a Native of France and Soldier of the French Revolution under Napoleon Bonaparte." And this one is dated November 15, 1846.

Once again the circumstances of Ney's death proved sufficiently cloudy to warrant the rise of "strange death" stories. Briefly, they were these.

Ney had been one of Napoleon's bravest and most trusted leaders. But when Napoleon abdicated, he promptly swore allegiance to Louis XVIII. On Napoleon's escape from Elba, he assured the king that he would capture Napoleon and bring him to Paris in an iron cage. But when he met Napoleon on the road at Lons-le-Saulnier, Ney's sentimental remembrance of old campaigns led him to embrace Napoleon and put his troops at the disposal of his old commander. Of course, that made Ney a traitor to the King and to the Allies in the campaign that followed. At Waterloo, Ney personally led several charges of the Old Guard right up to the British squares. But when the battle was lost, he promptly advocated the return of the Bourbons. Louis ordered his arrest on August 5, despite the fact that the Capitulation of Paris had offered amnesty to those who had fought for Napoleon.

Ney was a popular hero to the army and to the people. There was a feeling that he had been picked as a scapegoat out of many who were equally guilty, and some of his brother officers refused to sit at his court-martial, which did, however, convict him of treason. Even Wellington, by grace of whose Allied occupation troops Louis was reigning, is believed to have been indignant at Ney's sentence, but he was in a difficult position, and he refused to interfere officially. He was in a perfect position, however, to arrange or at least to tolerate a faked execution if he had wished to do so.

Louis, still indignant at Ney's defection, refused all appeals for the Marshal and insisted that sentence be carried out.

At about 9:00 A.M. on December 7, 1815, Ney was driven in a carriage to the Luxembourg Gardens, where a detachment of veteran soldiers had been waiting since 5:00 A.M. Ney alighted, marched straight to a wall, and turned to face the firing squad. He refused to have his eyes bandaged, asserted his innocence, and dramatically striking his hand to his heart, called on the soldiers to fire.

Ney fell. The official report says the body lay in place from

9:20 to 9:30. There was no *coup de grâce*. The body was then carried to the nearby Hospital for Foundlings, where it lay all day and all night. The next morning it was buried in the cemetery of Pere la Chaise.

Thus the official report. Yet one witness, Quentin Dick, an Irish member of the British Parliament, says the body was carried away in a carriage within three minutes, and that there was no medical examination. Only a month later, four Englishmen were prosecuted in France for helping another condemned man, General Lavalette, to escape, and at least one of them is known to have been a house guest of the Princesse de la Moskowa (Madame Ney). There is considerable conflicting testimony about the nature of the wounds on the body of the executed man. His wife did not attend the funeral; she did not honor his grave when in 1848 the change of government made this at last possible; she never remarried.

The four years between 1815 and 1819 are silent. They are explained by the thesis that Ney was quietly preparing himself by study for a career as schoolmaster. But in 1819 a man calling himself Peter Stuart Ney was recognized by French refugees in Georgetown, South Carolina, as Marshal Ney. He was known to have taught school at Brownsville, and then at Mocksville, North Carolina, in Mecklenburg County, Virginia, and from 1830 to his death in 1846 again in North Carolina. As Peter Ney he became well known, and many people believed him to be the Marshal. They knew him well for twenty-seven years, and they were convinced. More important, many Frenchmen testified similarly. The daughter of Pasqual Luciani, an old Napoleonic soldier settled in Montgomery, Alabama, made affidavit that her father came to America with Ney. Dr. E. M. C. Neyman of Indiana frequently said he was the son of Marshal Ney. A Colonel J. J. Lehmanowsky, a Polish officer under Napoleon, recognized Ney on the street in Knightstown, Indiana. Competent handwriting experts, including the David N. Carvalho whose expert testimony was so important in the Dreyfus case, declared that examples of writings by Marshal Ney and Peter Ney were written by the same hand. There is good evidence that Peter Ney fainted and fell to the floor on learning of Napoleon's death in 1821, and that he tried that same evening to commit suicide. On at least one occasion, Peter Ney proved himself to be an expert swordsman. He filled such books as he could find on the Napoleonic era with curt and pertinent written comments. He never presumed on the identity he claimed, but gained the respect of all who knew him by his simple manner of living in his role as schoolmaster.

On his deathbed he averred once again that he was Marshal Ney, and referred attendants to a manuscript in his desk which would establish the matter. It was found to be in a shorthand which no one could read. A visiting lecturer, Pliny Miles, borrowed the manuscript on representation that he would get a French scholar in New York to decipher it. But no translation, transcript, or reproduction of this manuscript has ever appeared.

Thus one can only say once again that the historical proofs are lacking. But equally, one cannot deny with absolute certainty that Michel Ney, Duke of Elchingen, Prince of Moskowa, and Marshal of France, lived a second life as Peter Stuart Ney, Carolina schoolmaster.

One of the best accounts of the Lost Dauphin, together with a study of other emigres to America during the Revolutionary period and afterward, is T. Wood Clark's *Emigres in the Wilderness* (N. Y., 1941). Those with a further interest in such things will find plentiful material in the works of Dr. Augustin Cabanes, a French physician who was one of the first to apply medical knowledge to biography and history in a systematic way. The skeptical and prolific Dr. Cabanes produced a dozen volumes on historical dubiousness, including *Les Morts Mysterieuses de l'Histoire* (Paris, 1901), four volumes of *Le Cabinet secret de l'Histoire* (Paris, 1895), and six more collected under the title *Legendes & Curiosites de l'Histoire* and *Les Indiscretions de l'Histoire* (Paris, 1903). The curious little book, *The Lost Dauphin*, by A. De Grasse Stevens (Sunnyside, England, 1887), is hard to obtain, but provides an interesting study.

One of the most detailed studies of the Ney problem is in *Fact, Fake or Fable*, by Rupert Furneaux (London, 1954), but the story is also well told in *The Bonapartes in America*, by Clarence Edward Macartney and Gordon Dorrance (Philadelphia, 1939). A highly detailed account of the last days of Marshal Ney in France will be found in James A. Weston's *Historic Doubts As to the Execution of Marshal Ney* (N.Y., 1895). The most recent and readable study is *Marshal Ney: A Dual Life*, by LeGette Blythe (N.Y., 1937), a Charlotte, N. Carolina, newspaperman who spent much time among the local sources and produced a most readable book.

Though there is a good deal too strange to be believed, nothing is too strange to have happened.

—THOMAS HARDY: *Notebooks*

Richard III and the Princes in the Tower

FOR FOUR HUNDRED YEARS THE very symbol of heartless cruelty, of devious ambition, of sheer black-hearted villainy, has been Richard III of England, "this poisonous hunch-back'd toad," "this lump of foul deformity."

Shakespeare made it so when he wrote his *The Tragedy of Richard Third* about 1593. Since then, generation after generation has shuddered at the plots and murders of Richard and heard his last desperate cry, "My kingdom for a horse!" as it rang from the lips of Irving, Booth, Forrest, Macready, Barrymore, Gielgud, and Olivier.

The events of the Wars of the Roses were no farther distant from Shakespeare than the Civil War is from us today. Yet here, as in so many cases, there is a great gulf between the thespian Richard of the play and the historical Richard who died on Bosworth Field in 1485.

History does not think quite so badly of Richard as did Shakespeare, and it thinks less badly of him as time goes on, especially recently, when friends have arisen to defend his name. There are, for instance, The Friends of Richard III, Inc., in America, the Fellowship of the White Boar in England, and the Richard III Society in Australia. Members of these associations are convinced that not merely Shakespeare, but history itself, has done wrong by Richard, and they want to see justice done a King whom they consider more sinned against than sinning.

It takes nothing from the glory of Shakespeare to say that his plays are better as plays than they are as history. In his relationship to Richard the essential facts are clear. Shakespeare worked up his historical background for the play from chronicles which were current at the time, especially Holinshed. It is well known that Holinshed based his account of Richard on Sir Thomas More, but even More was only eight years old when Richard died, so he had no personal acquaintance with the events. More made his career under Henry VII and Henry VIII, the Tudor successors to the last Plantagenet. But he grew up as a boy in the household of Cardinal Morton, a contemporary of Richard and one of his greatest enemies. It is not hard to guess where More learned about Richard. So Shakespeare's play is based on an account stemming from an enemy of Richard and written by an office-holder of the dynasty which overthrew and succeeded him. Shakespeare sends a terrible array of ghosts to plague Richard the night before Bosworth: Prince Edward, son of Henry VI, Henry VI himself, the Duke of Clarence, Rivers, Grey and Vaughan, Hastings, and finally the two young princes murdered in the Tower—all reproaching him with their deaths.

Even orthodox history has never accused Richard III of the deaths of all these. Of the deaths of Prince Edward and his father, Henry VI, and of that of the Duke of Clarence, he is almost surely innocent. But we are concerned here with the death of the little princes in the tower, "girdling one another within their alabaster innocent arms, their lips were four red roses on a stalk . . ." in Shakespeare's moving language.

These boys were twelve-year-old Edward, son and heir-apparent to King Edward IV, and his younger brother Richard, Duke of York. When their father, Edward IV, died in April, 1483, the boy Edward technically became king.

Richard was their uncle; that is, he was the brother of King Edward IV whom he had served loyally as general and administrator. But he disliked Elizabeth Woodville, Edward IV's Queen, who had filled the nobility and civil service with her kinsmen. When Edward IV died, there was an inevitable contest. Richard, who was appointed guardian of the two boys and Protector of the Realm during the young Prince Edward's minority, was, if able to exercise those powers, in a position to eliminate the Woodville influence entirely. But that ambitious and able family did not propose to be eliminated.

When Edward IV died, the young Prince of Wales, his heir, was physically with the Woodville faction, staying with Elizabeth Woodville's eldest brother, Lord Rivers, at Ludlow. The Woodville faction saw an opportunity to cling to power by ruling in the name of the Boy-King. They set out for London with the boy and two thousand armed men, giving every evidence of intending to govern.

Richard was at York at the time. He immediately called in such of the nobility as were within reach and swore their allegiance to the Boy-King as Edward V. With six hundred followers, he set out for London, intending, apparently, to meet his nephew, the Boy-King, and escort him to London, just what Rivers and Sir Richard Grey were already doing. The two parties met at Northampton. There Richard arrested both Rivers and Grey and took charge of the young princes. There is no sign that, up to the time they arrived in London, Richard had any intention but to protect the Prince, assure his coronation, and act as his Regent.

But about this time a matter was revealed which had remained until then a closely guarded secret. It was this: two or three years before he married Elizabeth Woodville (a widow with two children, and hence unacceptable as queen to many Englishmen), Edward IV had been formally betrothed to Lady Eleanor Butler (or Boteler). In the fifteenth century such a contract was almost as binding as marriage itself and remained so, even though Lady Eleanor later entered a convent. So there was a shadow over the marriage of Edward IV and Elizabeth Woodville—a shadow deep enough to make it possible to question the legitimacy of her children by Edward and to argue that they could not succeed to the crown.

Robert Stillington, Dean of St. Martin's and Keeper of the Privy Seal, revealed the facts publicly shortly after Richard arrived in London with the Boy-King and his younger brother. Stillington even claimed he had secretly married Edward and Eleanor, though there is no proof of this.

Less than a month later, Richard, Duke of Gloucester, assumed the crown as Richard III. He may have been conveniently convinced that the children were illegitimate and could not properly wear the crown. He may simply have been overcome by ambition and chosen to believe what it was profitable to believe. We do not know. In any event, Parliament was persuaded to accept the view that the Edward-Elizabeth Woodville marriage was invalid and that their children were not heirs to the crown. (In the following reign of Henry VII Parliament reversed itself.) However, the young princes being ruled out, Richard surely had the best claim, and after an impressive coronation, his brief two-year rule opened.

The opposition began to organize almost at once, gathering about the Woodvilles. They negotiated with a Lancastrian exile in Brittany, Henry Tudor, who had a very slender but tangible claim to the succession. An abortive revolt by the Duke of Buckingham, who had helped Richard gain the crown, was quickly suppressed, and Buckingham was beheaded on November 2, 1483. Fugitive nobles fled to France and gathered about Henry Tudor with French protection and support. At length he invaded England, gathering further support from his Welsh compatriots as he marched. Near Market Bosworth, the two forces met on August 22, 1485, and in a short but bloody battle Henry won the crown of England. It was found under a thorn tree where it had rolled after being hacked from the helmet of a beset Richard, who died of many wounds, fighting bravely to the last. His body was stripped and dishonored by the victor.

Henry Tudor became King under the style of Henry VII, and the line of Tudor kings was established, with the great era of Henry VIII and Elizabeth I which brought England into its destiny.

Henry knew that his title to the crown was not too impressive. He issued his first proclamations "By right of conquest and the Lancastrian blood" (putting conquest first). To solidify his claims and in an attempt to liquidate the York-Lancaster feud, he next married Elizabeth, daughter of Edward IV (January 18, 1486).

As Richard III had obligingly murdered the little princes, the normal heir of Edward IV was out of the way, and with his union with their sister, Henry was firmly on the throne. The little Crown Prince, Edward, had he been alive, might have been a threat to Henry. But he and his little brother were dead in the Tower. They had been a threat to Richard III, too, and he had eliminated them.

Or had he? Within a week after the victory at Bosworth Field, Henry Tudor was in London and in possession of the Tower. He certainly knew then whether the two little boys were still prisoners there or not. One of the first things Henry did was to draw up an Act of Attainder against Richard. Such an act is one by which a person is convicted of crimes and deprived of rights and standing without judicial trial. Henry, of course, wished to blacken the name and status of the dead Richard in order to strengthen his own position. In this act, Henry accused his predecessor of a long list of crimes, cruelties, and tyrannies. But there is no mention of the murder of the little princes in the Tower. Certainly that would have been a choice item to cite against Richard. But it is not even mentioned.

Those who defend Richard deduce from this telling omission that the princes were still alive when Henry took possession of London and the Tower, and that, therefore, they were not murdered by Richard or even during his brief reign. They then go on to suggest that Henry himself had good reason to wish the boys out of the way, as their claim to the throne was and would always be while they lived far better than his own. And the Richard-faction does not hesitate to suggest that the murderer of the little princes was not Richard, but Henry.

It is, generally speaking, true that most of the historical accounts of the death of the little princes were written under Tudor auspices. But it is not entirely true. There are accounts in the *Croyland Chronicle* and by one Roos, a contemporary, and it is likely, despite Henry's significant omission in his Act of Attainder, that suspicion was raised against Richard in his own time. It has been suggested that he could easily have allayed such suspicions by displaying the young princes in public if they were really alive and safe. At any rate this was not done.

But it remains true that the governing historical accounts of Richard are all Tudor. Polydore Virgil, even Shakespeare, wrote in Tudor times and under a natural instinct, if not under tangible pressures, to favor the ruling house. It would not be at all surprising to find these accounts less than fair to Richard. The principal historian of the time, Polydore Virgil, was practically a propagandist for the Tudor era, though he came to England from Italy in 1502 and could easily have talked to eyewitnesses if he had wished to do so. Sir Thomas More has a deservedly high reputation as a scholar. He was the author of the famous *Utopia* and was a friend of Erasmus. Anything over his name commands respect, and it is difficult to believe that he would deliberately have falsified his account of Richard III. So it has generally been accepted without reserve. Yet his *History of Richard the Thirde, Writen by Master Thomas More then one of the undersheriffs of London; about the year of our Lorde 1513* was the work of a rising young careerist under Henry VIII. It was first printed, in a corrupt text, in *Hardyinge's Chronicle* (1543) and *Halle's Chronicle* (1550) and in complete text in 1557. This latter was from a manuscript in his own handwriting, now lost. It may have been dictated by Cardinal Morton, or translated from his Latin. The manuscript was found among More's papers and had never been published by him or, indeed, until long after his death, thirty or more years after he wrote it.

It is interesting to note how the story-book picture of Richard stems from More's (or Morton's) account. Richard, he wrote, was "little of stature, ill fetured of limmes, croke backed, his left shoulder much higher than his right, hard favoured of visage . . . he was malicious, wrathfull, envious. . . . He was close and secrete, a deepe dissimuler, lowlye of counteynaunce, arrogant of heart, outwardly coumpinable where he inwardly hated, not letting to kisse whome hee thoughte to kill. . . ."

There is your Shakespearean villain, all made to order. More repeats the gossip that Richard had killed Henry VI and Clarence, but checks himself: "But of al this pointe is there no certaintie, and whoso divineth uppon conjectures maye as wel shote to farre as to short."

He is explicit about the murder of the young princes, yet even here he admits that there were some who doubted: "But as he finished his time with the beste death, and the most righteous, that is to wyt his own; so began he with the most piteous and wicked, I meane the lamentable murther of his innocent nephewes, the young king and his tender brother. Whose death and final infortune hathe natheles so far comen in question, that some remain yet in doubt, whither they wer in his dayes destroyde or no."

More probably refers here to the rise of Perkin Warbeck, the unhappy youth who claimed to be the prince, Edward IV's son, and who had enough believers in him to raise a small rebellion around his authority. At least the people who believed in Warbeck did not believe he had been murdered by Richard or anyone else. And there must have been others, as More admits.

Even More's uncomplimentary personal description of Richard does not go the limit. As an illustration of how great an effort was made to blacken his name, witness the stories that he was born feet-first after a two-year pregnancy of his mother, and that he came into the world with all his teeth, and hair to his shoulders. Nonsense of this kind certainly suggests a conscious effort to blacken Richard's name, to make him appear a veritable monster.

No one can be sure that More's account is in fact Morton's, but he passed much of his youth in Morton's household, and Morton was Richard's deadly enemy. It would certainly be quite natural that More should depend on a personal mentor and eyewitness for accounts of what went on when he was himself a boy of five or even younger. And to the extent that More's account depends on Morton, it is certainly biased.

The picture drawn by More and others of Richard as a hunchback and cripple does not square at all with his unquestioned prowess at arms, any more than it does with the testimony of other contemporaries or with his pictures. It seems likely that he was unsymmetrically developed, but no twisted cripple could swing mace and broadsword as Richard unquestionably did. There is testimony that he was pronouncedly good-looking and attractive to women. The melodramatic wooing of Anne Neville, widow of Prince Edward, on her way to the funeral of the slain Henry VI, as portrayed by Shakespeare in Act I, Scene 2, of the play, is pure fiction. There is no reason to believe Richard was responsible for their deaths, and he was clearly very much in love with Anne, whom he had known since childhood.

As a matter of fact, Richard's career, right up to the death of his brother, Edward IV, was admirable. The fact that he was in the north when Edward died, and took almost a month to come to London, does not argue a man consumed with ambition to usurp the crown. When he did come south, and met the Woodvilles at Northampton, he first learned that the Marquis of Dorset, brother of Elizabeth Woodville, had already seized the king's treasure and equipped a navy. Surely at that point he had every reason to believe that the Woodvilles intended a coup, and his arrest of Rivers and Grey was more or less justified.

Yet ambition may well have taken root at this very moment, and the rest of his misdeeds are then not impossible, even if one rules out the concept of a base villain plotting from the very beginning.

The simple truth is that we do not know for certain when, or by whose hand and order, the little princes died in the Tower. Their deaths would have been a convenience either to Richard III or Henry VII. Both had the opportunity and the power to decree it; either would have been quite capable of it. For it must be remembered that both these were men of the late Renaissance, when power went to him who could hold it, and the liquidation of those who might contest that power was a regular tactic of high politics and an occupational hazard of every man of birth and position. Richard may not have ordered the princes' murder, but he did not hesitate summarily to liquidate Hastings, Rivers, Grey, and even his close collaborator, Buckingham. Henry VII was scarcely less ruthless. He let Stillington and John of Gloucester (Richard's illegitimate son) die in prison, and executed Warwick, Clarence's son. He shut Elizabeth Woodville up in a nunnery and seized all her possessions. He arrested and executed without trial Sir James Tyrrel, the supposed agent of Richard in the murder of the princes, and it may be significant that the first "official" accounts of Tyrrel's part in the murders appeared shortly after his execution.

Certainly either Richard III or Henry VII was quite capable of the twin murder in the Tower, just as almost any reigning monarch of the close of the fifteenth century would have been capable of it. But history can give no final, air-tight answer. Evidence is lacking that would prove either man guilty beyond a reasonable doubt.

The basic account to read here (after Shakespeare himself, of course) is More. James Gairdner in the *History of the Life and Reign of Richard the Third* (Cambridge, 1898) began with a youthful suspicion, stimulated by Walpole's *Historical Doubts*, that Richard was comparatively innocent. After long research for his book, he concludes that he was probably guilty. But C. R. Markham, in his *Richard III* (London, 1906), is less certain. Hugh Ross Williamson, in *Historical Whodunits* (London and N.Y., 1955), exonerates Richard and lays the guilt at the door of Henry VII. One of the most readable discussions is in Josephine Tey's *Daughter of Time* (N.Y., 1952). Here a police inspector, laid up in hospital, idly studies a picture of Richard III, speculates on whether this is a guilty face or not, and then begins to read the sources. One is pleasantly led down a review of the case to a conclusion that Richard III was a much-maligned man.

This is the point of view of the Friends of Richard III, Inc., an organization of some 160 or more members who have made the rehabilitation of the name of Richard III a sort of hobby. The head of the organization is Alexander Clark, 321 East 43d Street, New York City. The purposes of the society are to "disprove the calumnies against the character of the last Plantagenet king; to see that such misrepresentations are no longer perpetuated in text books and histories," as well as eventually to help in the restitution of the College of Arms in London, founded and chartered by Richard.

A good study is the *Memoirs of Richard III*, by John Heneage Jesse (Boston, 1862), though not memoirs in the ordinary sense of the word. *The Tragic King*, by Philip Lindsay (N. Y., 1934), and *The Plantagenets*, by John Harvey (N.Y., 1948), are helpful. A new life, rather favorable to Richard, by Paul Murray Kendall, appeared in 1956, but was not yet available at the time this was written. It is interesting that Winston Churchill, in the first volume of his *History of the English-Speaking Peoples* (London and N. Y., 1956), holds to the traditional view, rejects all revisionism as to Richard, and says that "it will take many ingenious books to raise this issue to the dignity of a historical controversy."

None the less the controversy continues, and there are few more fascinating subjects for a little amateur historical research.

Abraham Lincoln's Letter to Mrs. Bixby

On Thanksgiving Day, 1864, Adjutant-General William Schouler of Massachusetts called at the home of Mrs. Lydia Bixby, widow, of 15 Dover Street, Boston. His mission was to deliver a Thanksgiving dinner, a gift of money from the people of Boston, and a letter.

The letter was as follows:

EXECUTIVE MANSION
Washington, November 21, 1864.
Mrs. Bixby, Boston, Massachusetts.
Dear Madam:

I have been shown in the files of the War Department a statement of the Adjutant-General of Massachusetts that you are the mother of five sons who have died gloriously on the field of battle. I feel how weak and fruitless must be any words of mine which should attempt to beguile you from the grief of a loss so overwhelming. But I cannot refrain from tendering to you the consolation that may be found in the thanks of the Republic they died to save. I pray that our Heavenly Father may assuage the anguish of your bereavement, and leave you only the cherished memory of the loved and lost, and the solemn pride that must be yours to have laid so costly a sacrifice upon the altar of freedom.

Yours very sincerely and respectfully,
Abraham Lincoln.

The widow Bixby, having made this brief and shadowy bow, retires from the pages of history. Perhaps it is just as well, for such searches as have been made into her life are not reassuring. They suggest that she was not merely of a very humble, but perhaps of a not too respectable position in life. But it does not matter. All the more credit, perhaps, to a president who took time to write in this way to a very inconspicuous woman who had certainly suffered much. What matters is the letter.

And Adjutant-General Schouler, who had been entrusted by the White House with delivering the letter, took the precaution of copying it verbatim and giving out the text to the newspapers. It was widely reprinted all over the country, arousing mixed reactions. Papers supporting the Civil War and Lincoln acclaimed it as a majestic statement of the nation's sympathy for those who had supported it at great sacrifice. But there were papers of the opposition who did not hesitate to call it a cheap bid for sympathy and a maudlin piece of demagoguery. Nevertheless it took firm root in the hearts of the people, and it has been reproduced almost as often as the Gettysburg Address itself.

The circumstances that gave rise to the letter were these: In September there had come to Lincoln's desk a letter from Governor Andrew of Massachusetts in behalf of Mrs. Bixby. Andrew passed on information from Schouler that Mrs. Bixby's five sons had, every one, been killed on the field of battle. Because Mrs. Bixby was in need, she had been aided by Governor Andrew and others. Lincoln had Governor Andrew's letter before him at least by early October, and his letter to Mrs. Bixby was not written until late November. Those facts acquit him of the charge, made by his political opponents, that he had written and used the letter for political purposes.

After its personal delivery by White House order to Mrs.

Bixby, what became of the actual letter itself? Nobody knows. The original letter sent from the White House has never been found. There is no lack of alleged facsimiles, differing materially from one another, but no original letter from which such facsimiles could have been made has ever turned up, though it has been sought as no other letter in history. There is no reason to question the text in the form in which it was preserved through the copy which Schouler made for the newspapers. Lincoln's son, Robert, used to be pestered from time to time by people wanting to sell him the "original" of the letter, but he never saw one which he thought had any claim to being genuine. There have been various rumors that the original was in certain museums, at Oxford or in the Morgan Library in New York, but inquiry always fails to produce it.

In the early nineteen-twenties, perhaps the most careful student of Lincoln, preparing for the *Life* he was to write, was Dr. William E. Barton. Among other matters, Dr. Barton undertook to look painstakingly into the whole matter of the Bixby letter. He wrote a magazine article on his findings, but found difficulty in getting it printed, the editors feeling that the public did not want to have its faith in a beautiful story disturbed.

But Dr. Barton persisted. He researched the army archives for the record of the five Bixby boys. He found that Charles had indeed been killed at Fredericksburg, and Oliver at Petersburg. But Henry, reported killed at Gettysburg, was found to have been captured, exchanged, and returned to his mother in good health. George was taken prisoner and then enlisted as a Confederate soldier, his record showing the damning entry "deserted to the enemy." Edward, the youngest, listed as eighteen years old, but whose mother said he was only sixteen, had enlisted, but had then deserted and gone to sea.

Heaven knows that by any standard this widow had given enough, lost enough. But the new discoveries tended to becloud, just a little, the perfection of the story. But not that of the letter. There is no reason to believe that anyone, from Governor Andrew down through Adjutant-General Schouler to the President himself had acted in less than complete good faith. It was, suggested Dr. Barton, "a beautiful blunder and well worth while for the sake of the letter."

But this was not the end. In 1940 there appeared the memoirs of Dr. Nicholas Murray Butler, long-time president of Columbia University. The book, *Across the Busy Years,* carried authority, for Dr. Butler had also been president of the American Academy of Arts and Letters, and a prominent figure in the literary, educational and political worlds. It is hard to discount this statement in the book, made in the most deliberate and precise language: "It is now possible to make public the fact that the famous Bixby letter . . . was not written by Abraham Lincoln at all, but by John Hay."

John Hay had been, as a young man, Lincoln's private secretary. There is no question that he helped the President materially in preparing various papers. It may even be, as Butler suggested, that he was capable of imitating Lincoln's handwriting, though he is not known to have done so. But Hay was a poet and an able writer, sitting daily in the shadow of Lincoln and under the spell of his words as he wrote and spoke them. Under such circumstances it is hard to call it impossible that he might have composed a letter in what is so unmistakably the Lincoln style.

The manner in which Butler learned the story was this: he was a friend of Lord John Morley, the British politician. They met in London in 1912 and Morley told him the story under injunction never to reveal it until Morley was dead. He had been, Morley related, a guest at the White House during the Theodore Roosevelt administration, and had been deeply moved by a facsimile of the Bixby letter which was framed and hung in his bedroom. Happening to visit John Hay, then Secretary of State, the following day, he mentioned his admiration for the letter. Hay "listened with a quizzical look on his face" and then told Morley that he himself had written the Bixby letter. He asked Morley to treat the matter as confidential until after Hay's death. Morley later passed the story to Butler under the same injunction. When the death of both men had released him from his obligation, Butler published the story in 1940.

It is evidence that can not be disregarded. But is it conclusive? The story is oral, and at third-hand, though all three men are reliable witnesses, and Butler sets it down at length without doubt and with deliberate gravity. Yet all were relying on memory alone, and there is always a possibility of misunderstanding. J. G. Randall cites Hay's own diary to suggest that at the time of his interview with Morley he was distraught because of the death of a brother, and may not have been at his most thoughtful. There is always a possibility that Hay, his attention drawn to the facsimile which Morley had seen, was thinking primarily of that, and meant only to say that he had *manually* written the letter, perhaps from a corrected draft or even from dictation by Lincoln. Though Butler had no doubt in the matter, it is still possible that in this oral relay over many years, Hay to Morley to Butler, misunderstanding may have crept in.

Yet there can be no doubt that to Dr. Barton's "beautiful blunder" there has been added the distinct possibility that Lincoln never wrote the letter at all. The fact that the original has never been found, that the existing facsimiles are unquestionably made from forgeries, makes it impossible to apply the usual handwriting tests.

Even if the original letter should some day be discovered, and should be found to be in Hay's handwriting rather than

Lincoln's, it might prove only that what Hay meant was that he transcribed it manually.

And yet, whoever wrote it and under whatever misapprehensions, there stands the text of the letter, unchanged, unshaken, and immortal.

Sole authority, though an excellent one, for the Hay version of the Bixby story is in Vol. 2 of Nicholas Murray Butler's *Across the Busy Years* (N.Y., 1940). The best discussion since the appearance of that book, weighing its evidence, is in *Lincoln the President—The Last Full Measure*, by J. G. Randall and Richard N. Current (N.Y., 1955). Randall thinks the Butler story insufficiently grounded, and is unshaken in his belief that Lincoln wrote the letter. There are detailed studies of the Bixby affair by F. Lauriston Ballard, Sherman Day Wakefield, and Kendall Banning, but they are neither completely up to date nor easy to find.

The best single account with which to begin is, as usual, Carl Sandburg's *Abraham Lincoln*, Vol. 3 of *The War Years*, but this appeared before the Butler revelations. Barton's investigation is best seen in his two-volume *Life of Abraham Lincoln* (Indianapolis, 1925).

No normal human being wants to hear the truth.
—H. L. MENCKEN: *Prejudices*, 6th Series,
"Hymn to the Truth"

History and the Media

Is HISTORY, AFTER ALL, IMPORTANT? If it were a mere game, a "who-dun-it" played at the scholarly level with real characters, there would be nothing to history that Dorothy L. Sayres and S. S. Van Dine have not done better. If all the hair-splitting and document-examination and critical evaluation were nothing more than merely to elevate one scholar to the discredit of another, were nothing more than a laborious development of insignificant details, it would not be worth the trouble.

But there is more to the study and the reading of history than that. History has, in the long run, the same objective as literature—to help us better to understand life. It approaches this objective by a different technique, and it builds its structure with different materials. This is not to argue for a moment that one structure is stronger or more dependable than the other. It is merely to say that they are different.

There has arisen during this twentieth century (as it has arisen before, in ages which we like to call "dark") a pronounced anti-intellectualism, a feeling that both studies and literature are not merely vain, but somehow untrustworthy. To people swayed by this feeling, there is little use in arguing either for history or literature, or for poetry or music or the arts in general. I am talking to the others.

To the others, there is still faith that any civilization worthy of the name must be grounded in a ceaseless pursuit of truth. Whether truth be sought through study or through the arts makes no difference. Any pursuit of truth is not only worthwhile, it is the foundation-stone of civilization. The study and reading of history is one of those approaches to truth. It is only one; all the arts and sciences are such approaches. All have their place; all are good. And each touches upon all the others. They are not air-tight compartments. It is only in a few institutions afflicted by mental arteriosclerosis that events like the Industrial Revolution are preempted entirely either by the historians, the social-scientists, or the physical scientists. Is *Pepys' Diary* history or sociology or literature? It is only within the past hundred years that historians have found that what people have done in literature and art is a part of their history. Books like *Uncle Tom's Cabin, Ten Nights in a Bar-Room,* and *The Crisis* have themselves helped to make history. Even at the moment when scientific investigation becomes more and more specialized, and the historian concentrates more and more fiercely on periods and episodes, it is becoming clearer to the layman that all this is part of one whole. Even at a time when textbooks are being written to introduce to the theoretical physicist his brethren who are working as chemists or engineers on perhaps the same problem, the layman stands far enough clear of all this specialization to see the whole perhaps even better than the specialists. Between history, and biography, and the arts and sciences, and even journalism, who shall draw air-tight distinctions? Not laymen. Is not yesterday's newspaper history, and may it not be literature?

But to return to history. History is simply the story of the past as reconstructed from the evidence. In the best histories, there is a subjective attempt to seek broad truth. But such interpretation must be that of a good mind operating on a base of all the facts that can be found.

That is why there is sometimes a good deal of bedevilment when the paths of history and literature cross. For with literature, there enters a new set of values, romantic and dramatic values. The historian is by no means bound to ignore these. But he is bound to make them secondary to what the best research shows to have "actually happened." For the novelist, the dramatist, the radio and television producer, the romantic and dramatic elements are bound to come first.

Who has not watched the cheapest sort of moving picture play, furtively hiding the tears stinging in his eyes, and then met, dry-eyed and dumb, the same tragedy in his own life? This is because life is never pure drama—there are always the dishes to wash after the funeral. It is also because life seems dramatic only at second-hand, a sort of spectator-life. There is great drama in war, but not to the men who are fighting it, while they are fighting. The essence of drama is in watching life, not in living it.

That is why, for instance, in Shakespeare's historical plays, the characters talk as though they were withdrawn and watching their own careers unfold. Nobody pretends, when he watches *Henry the Fourth*, *Richard the Third*, *Julius Caesar*, or *Antony and Cleopatra*, that "this is how it happened." Drama being drama, he must say "this is how historic characters might have thought, and talked, and acted had they been able to stand off and watch their own lives." Further, the dramatist is under no obligation to be accurate with history. Shakespeare, writing for a Tudor England, is not only under the necessity of giving the Tudors all the best of it; his first obligation is to the show. Shaw, giving us his mischievous little Cleopatra and his avuncular Caesar, is merely having fun with characters who happened to have a historical existence as well. Any resemblance to real historical characters is purely coincidental.

Thus the inevitable difference between the stage, the movies, the novel, and history. The former are concerned with the dramatic elements of life, distilled out of it and presented to detached viewers or readers. The historian is concerned with what happened, and with how and why it happened, with no obligation at all to weep for Hecuba.

This is not to say that the moment historical events are subjected to purely literary treatment Clio is necessarily and foully ravaged. The novelist may find within the authenticated material of history all the romance and all the drama he needs. But the point is, he needs it. And many a novelist has seen fit to ignore or even to pervert the known facts when they failed easily to supply the necessary drama or romance. The novelist Charles Burdett can make Aaron Burr say to Margaret Moncrieffe, "I can give no better proof of my love than I have done by sacrificing honor, duty, morality, and all, to love—I do so love you, Margaret." If the novelist cannot prove that Burr said it, neither can I prove that he did not. Based on what is known of Burr, I reserve the right to say that I think it highly unlikely.

But that is fictionized biography at its worst. At its best, you have works like Gertrude Atherton's *The Conqueror*, a portrait of Alexander Hamilton. Mrs. Atherton actually began her research on Hamilton with the idea of writing a straight biography, but was carried away by some of the dramatic aspects and turned it into a novel. But all the research incident to the writing of a biography had already gone into it. Or take Catherine Drinker Bowen's magnificent *Yankee from Olympus*, which, though she calls it "deliberately embellished," forms in fact a happy conjunction of readability with the most carefully accurate scholarship. Poetry, on the scale of Stephen Vincent Benét's great epic of the Civil War, *John Brown's Body*, can give a truer feeling of the time than many a history, and even Longfellow's *Evangeline* pictures vividly the expulsion of the Acadians from Nova Scotia.

History, even at schoolbook level, has always held up Benedict Arnold as a very synonym for the word "traitor." The reader of Kenneth Roberts' novels, *Arundel* and *Rabble in Arms*, wherein Arnold is vividly presented in his younger and more heroic days, might form a distinctly different impression. For Roberts' admiration for this phase of Arnold's life led him to excuse and palliate his later treachery, making it seem not merely pardonable, but perhaps "all for the best." Fortunately, the discovery of the British Headquarters correspondence of General Clinton made it possible in 1941 for Carl Van Doren to tell the story of Arnold's treason in detail never possible before, and he did it in *Secret History of the American Revolution* (N.Y., 1941). Nothing can obliterate Arnold's youthful heroism at Quebec and Saratoga, but the *Secret History* leaves no doubt at all, with its full array of authentic Arnold and André letters, that Arnold for sixteen months before his final desertion had been haggling with the British over his price—the whole transaction was carried on at a despicable and degrading level, as were others of his transactions. Arnold was no "disillusioned hero honestly converted to the enemy," but a crafty, unscrupulous, and ignoble scoundrel. The schoolbooks were right all the time. Roberts' purely fictional characters are splendid, and the historical background against which they operate is accurate, well researched, and graphic. But for actual historical characters, one does better to turn to history.

There is a long list of historical novels which are well worth reading even by one who is primarily interested in history, for many of them have been done with scrupulous care as to events and the manner of living of the people concerned. As in any field, the trick is to choose the best, with the warning signal always up.

Thus, while historical novels at their best can often produce a true picture based on careful research (Tolstoy's *War and Peace* is perhaps the best existing picture of the Russian campaign in the Napoleonic Wars), yet they are not intended to be relied on in detail, and at their worst they represent an arrogant perversion of real people and real events to make a corrosively false bit of entertainment.

The drama, being largely dialogue, must perforce, in presenting historical events, invent words for the tongues of historical characters, for which the best that can be said is: "This is what George Washington or Abraham Lincoln might have said under certain circumstances." The more conscientious of playwrights can, by careful study of known and actual words and writings, invent dialogues which *may* have great verisimilitude. If the character is really understood through sound study and investigation, perhaps little violence is done. But always remember that there may be history without drama, but there is no drama without dramatics.

Two centuries ago, people read history. Macauley, Froude, Gibbon, and, later on, Prescott, Parkman, and Bancroft were read as no historian is read today. Considering the vast growth in the literate population, no twentieth-century historian has equaled the following of those of the eighteenth and nineteenth centuries. Leaders—the men who exercised power in England, say—read history. Well down into the nineteenth century it was understood that anyone pretending to hope for political power must be deeply read in history. Washington, Jefferson, Adams, Madison—all the Founding Fathers—read history. Wilson taught it. Theodore Roosevelt wrote it. Hoover made at Stanford one of the greatest modern collections of it. Even Truman, not a "literary" man, turned out to have studied history a great deal more widely than most people had expected. And, of course, Winston Churchill, one of the greatest leaders in action the modern era has produced, not only was steeped in history from birth, but has written as well as made history.

Since World War II there has been a pronounced tendency to turn again to history. Gibbon outsells everything else in the Viking Portable series. Tacitus and Herodotus are high on the Penguin list and Prescott still sells briskly in the Modern Library. Toynbee, Russell, and Northrop have been best-sellers, and the history and biography of the Civil War period have vied with the flood of memoirs describing the period surrounding World War II. Magazines like *Life* have made some serious and praiseworthy efforts to popularize history.

But despite all this, even the college-educated person in the United States is apt to be lamentably ignorant of the barest outline of the past. As for those of even less formal education, they are likely to have been left to form their ideas from a few novels and a torrent of half-baked movies and television shows which tend to compress all history into a series of love affairs against a background of appropriate mood-music. History is apt to be a vague parade of people who looked a good deal like George Arliss, Paul Muni, Charles Laughton, or Marlon Brando, and there are circles in which a telephone is still (1956) called an "Ameche." The "love conquers all" theme has furnished many historical novelists with a sword to cut all too easily the Gordian knots of history.

And yet all this is important, for today we have cast our lot with popular government. What people think, what masses of people think, guides policy as never before. What they think of their past is bound to influence what they think of their present and their future. So it is important that to these ineffective or even meretricious dabs at history there are being added some notable exceptions, even in the newer media. When Omnibus presented on television its exemplary series *The Adams Family*, with Allan Nevins as commentator and general supervisor, or again offered its series on *The Constitution*, with Joseph Welch guiding the narration, every effort was made to confine dialogue to known words of the speakers, to hold historic events within the channels in which they are known to have run. Yet even Omnibus had to present a short "rebuttal" program to satisfy those who felt that James Agee's version of Lincoln and Ann Rutledge had overrun the known facts. For this story, brimming with poignant suffering and sadness, has become a part of the American tradition. Yet the plain fact is that we know very little about it that can be said with certainty. None the less, these and many similar programs have made gallant efforts to reconcile the demands of a mass audience with the demands of historical discipline. Such efforts to bring real history painlessly and yet without distortion to the people are almost beyond praise.

Some are being made available on film so that they may be repeated to other audiences than those who were able to see the original production. Columbia Broadcasting Company's *You Are There* has been placed on film, and even on 16 mm. film, as have been such subjects as "The Hamilton-Burr Duel," "Susan B. Anthony Is Tried for Voting," "Barnum Presents Jenny Lind," and similar dramatized slices of history. *You Are There* has seemed to me a little over-dramatized, but still, some effort has been made to keep to the historical record and not merely use history as a springboard to leap into dramatics. Allan Nevins and the Society of

American Historians have collaborated in a whole series of scripts called *The American Story*. Even the commercial movie industry produces an occasional biographical or historical drama, like *Zapata*, from which one comes away with a feeling, "yes, it must have been very like this."

A word might be said at this point of one source of historical evidence not hitherto available. That is the phonograph record and the tape recording. Instances are the series *I Can Hear It Now*, edited by Edward R. Murrow and Fred Friendly, which allows one to hear voices of principals and sound effects of events selected from the years 1919-1949. Elmer Davis has edited another such series, *Then Came War: 1939*, in which the voices of the major actors in that era may be heard. What we have not yet seen, but what is perfectly feasible technically, is the tampering with a taped recording so as to falsify it while giving auditors the impression that they are hearing the actual sounds as originally launched into the air. Even the apparently air-tight evidence of tape recordings will have to be carefully guarded to avoid the same pitfalls that have beset the manuscript itself.

Yet history must be brought to the people at every level, from the most exacting scholarly level to the more popular media insofar as they can transmit it without transmuting it into something else. For it is perfectly clear that democracy cannot be made to work by people who do not understand it. French politics and policies of today cannot be understood by people who never heard of the French Revolution. Why does Communist Russia re-write that country's entire history, and even revise it with every change in current policy? Because even the most contemporary-minded cannot deny that we are at any given moment the product of all we have been, and even the bubbles and ripples of the day's events float on a mighty stream of a continuous tradition from the past.

Interesting studies of the historical validity of certain popular historical novels have been made. One of these is by Max Farrand on S. Weir Mitchell's *Hugh Wynne* in the *Washington Historical Quarterly*, I (1906-07), and another by Grace L. Nute on Kenneth Roberts' *Northwest Passage* in *Minnesota History*, XIX (1938). For a general study, see *The American Historical Novel*, by E. E. Leisy (Norman, 1950), which displays the whole panorama of American history as seen through the eyes of the novelists. A similar survey, not only for the United States but for all countries, is in Ernest A. Baker's *History in Fiction* (London and N.Y., n.d.). This two-volume survey considers all novels in a costume or period setting as historical novels; some consider as such only those which are chiefly concerned with the activities of real characters and with real events. The chapter "Arms and the Woman," in Gilbert Highet's *A Clerk of Oxenford* (N.Y., 1954), is an amusing discussion of historical fiction technique, especially as applied to a Napoleonic romance called *Désirée*.

Aaron Burr is one of the most fascinating of American historical characters. Margaret Moncrieffe wrote her own memoirs (*Memoirs of Mrs. Coughlin*, New York, 1795), and while she gave herself the best of it, the contrast between her stark story and the romantic version of Charles Burdett in his novel *Margaret Moncrieffe* (N. Y., 1860) is illustrative. Burr's "Conspiracy" is an example of one of those matters on which 150 years of study has produced no agreement. Walter Flavius McCaleb, in *The Aaron Burr Conspiracy* (N. Y., 1936), musters a good deal of evidence against anything treasonable. There are several recent lives of Burr.

The Federal Communications Commission maintains files of recordings and broadcast scripts, and the Office of Education at Washington has issued a *Catalogue of Radio Recordings*, listing recordings of permanent value. The offices of national networks will usually give information about material they have.

For those who feel in general a lack of background in history, yet who hesitate to venture into so vast a field without some guidance, let me suggest Allan Nevins' *The Gateway to History* (N. Y., 1938) and (especially for English interest) A. L. Rowse's *The Use of History* (London, 1946).

A good example of movie and TV treatment of history is their versions of the tragedy at Mayerling in which Archduke Rudolph of Austria and his mistress, Maria Vetsera, came to their deaths. All such romanticized versions are based on the already romanticized novel of Claude Anet, called *Idyll's End*, and have only the sketchiest relation to such facts as are known.

The next time you see a biographical or historical movie or TV play, or read a historical novel, read a copy of the best biography you can find of the same subject, or the best historical account of the events in which the novel is set. It will be a rewarding experience.

Surely an historian's object should not be to amaze his readers by a series of thrilling anecdotes, nor should he aim to produce speeches which might have been delivered, nor to study dramatic propriety in detail like a writer of tragedy. On the contrary, his function is, above all, to record with fidelity what was actually said or done, no matter how commonplace it may be.

—POLYBIUS, 2nd century B.C.,
as quoted by James Harvey Robinson
in *The New History*

ONE SOMETIMES FINISHES A book of this kind with a hopeless feeling of "What *can* a man believe? . . . Can one believe *anything?*"

Of course one can. We have been making a tour along the rough edges of history, inspecting the slum-quarter, so to speak. But history at its best, through the painstaking labor of centuries of study, is close enough to truth to be a practical guide. And as long as study is free, it will continue to get closer to the truth, year by year, step by step.

Nevertheless it is good to have a point of view which questions everything. For then there gradually comes a realization that while it is not given to human beings to achieve absolute and final truth about human events, they have been given something almost as precious. It is the gift of curiosity, the instinct to keep everlastingly on the trail of truth, even if the quarry is never quite run to earth.

Then comes the ultimate realization that it is precisely this continual pursuit of truth that lifts men a little higher than the beasts and only a little lower than the angels. The faith that lies in honest doubt by no means precludes belief, nor paralyzes action based on belief. It means only that one acts at any time on the best belief he has been able to form up to that time. It may be (and one hopes it is) different from the belief he held when he was twelve.

Old beliefs, old truths, are shaken, and they fall. Newer, stronger, better beliefs take their place, ready to yield in turn to others if they present a stronger and better claim.

That is the way with history. That is the way with life, too.

Index